Perfect
CATS

Perfect CATS

Peter Warner

Sidgwick & Jackson Limited
London

First published in Great Britain in 1991 by
Sidgwick & Jackson Limited

Copyright © 1991 by Peter Warner

ISBN 0-283-06049-2

Typeset by Rowland Phototypesetting Limited
Bury St Edmunds, Suffolk

Printed in Italy by
Amilcare Pizzi, Milan

for Sidgwick & Jackson Limited
18–21 Cavaye Place
London SW10 9PG

for
Janet, John and Rachmaninov,
Django and Oliver, and my long-suffering dogs.

Contents

Foreword

Peter Warner has been described as the best feline artist of our time; and there is certainly no one better qualified to produce this exquisite collection of paintings of the world's domestic cats.

Perfect Cats represents a 'first': for there has never been a cat book quite like this, where the most important statements about the cats are made in the paintings and the text plays the supporting role, rather than the other way round.

Peter's expertise comes from a combination of natural talent, sensitivity towards the feline personality and minutely accurate attention to detail. In all his work is reflected a love of cats which is clearly returned by the cats themselves. When he visited my cat family to research this book it was obvious that he had been elected 'honorary cat', and he spent many hours among them, recording details of their posture and movement and allowing them to climb all over him in the process.

This book is the result of his many hours of painstaking research and analysis, not only of my cats but of cats owned by other breeders; and I feel sure it will become a source of reference for cat lovers for many years to come.

Cats from many countries have been included, some of which may be new to cat lovers and many of which are already well known worldwide. Some of the breeds, such as the Persian and the Siamese, are so well known that they hardly need further description, while others such as the Siberian and the Seychellois have previously been seen only by a privileged few. But Peter Warner's paintings, even of the well known breeds, have an instant appeal and offer a great deal of new information because they are representations of perfection rather than simply being pictures of cats.

The domestic cat is biologically the most perfect cat of all and has been described as the most successful carnivore in the world. It evolved from races of wildcat, and readily adapted to the diet and habits imposed by its close proximity to the human race, even adapting differently to the customs of humans in different parts of the world.

In general cat breeds originating from the domestic cats of warmer climates are more sinuous, noisier and more active than those originating from domestic cats of colder climates. The latter are more economical with movement, quieter and more stockily built. This book portrays them all, from the domestic cat, which can be described as a poem of moderation, to the extremes of stockiness seen in the Persian and the extremes of slenderness seen in the Siamese.

The cat fancy measures quality by good looks as well as personality, and good looks are judged by a set of standards known variously as 'breed standards' or 'standards of points'. In some associations there are even standards of excellence for the mongrels or 'moggies' and these include requirements for cleanliness and temperament. While Peter Warner's paintings can be fairly described as perfect representations of the breeds described in these standards, individual breeds and individual cats within breeds may not be perfect.

If a perfect cat is to be defined as one that is biologically sound and viable, attractive to the eye and a loving pet in the home then certainly not all cats are perfect. Whereas, in the human race, imperfections of conformation and personality are largely due to influences caused by the human race itself, the imperfections found in cats are outside their control, having been imposed on them by their owners and protectors.

The fact that leading magazines for cat lovers now feature regular contributions from 'cat psychologists' reflects the damage done to the domestic cat by an unthinking human race; and the fact that one of the most important cat fancy organizations in the world has found it necessary to appoint a top veterinary surgeon to speak to an assembly of delegates from twenty-six nations on the dangers of breeding to extremes of type underlines the extent of the damage done to the cat by human whims and fashions.

Peter Warner has faithfully recorded perfection in cats as specified in the breed standards and although he says that he is not in agreement with some of the requirements of standards he has, nevertheless, managed to translate their word pictures into a set of paintings that every cat lover can enjoy.

PAT TURNER. *Milton Keynes 1990.*

Introduction

I have admired cats for a long time. Their mobile form is always challenging to understand, but often elusive under camouflage. This is life painting with fur on!

Curiosity has bred in me an intense interest in cats' natural history, especially of the wild species, but it is the paradox of the cat that fascinates me most of all – the forward impetus but backward looking of the curious cat, the instant transformation from indolent repose to super-awareness, from sinuous companion to supreme hunter, effortless gambol to measured stalk and decisive sprint, all with innate dignity and ineffable equilibrium.

Felis catus, the domesticated cat, has four times as many varieties as any of the thirty-seven species of wild cat has sub-species, or races. This book is about these races, or breeds. All cats, wild and domestic, are remarkably similar, as befits the perfectly designed land hunter. One readily sees the tiger in the hearth, but who would recognize the wolf in the Pekingese?

In determining which breeds to illustrate, I decided to include only those which are recognized by at least one cat association, thus indicating that they have an enduring record, and breed true. This meant excluding one or two like the Californian Spangled Cat, which has not yet achieved any recognition, and very new breeds whose future is still uncertain.

My division of the breeds into groups is a logical one, based loosely on Cat Association of Britain principles. A breed is determined by differences in conformation, not by colour or pattern.

I could not attempt to show every colour and pattern of every breed – that would be too repetitive – but the majority of colours and patterns are illustrated. Many breeds are in their 'original' colours, whilst new colours have been introduced too, thus allowing the reader's imagination to extrapolate say a seal point Siamese from the blue point Siamese and seal point Birman illustrated here.

My pictorial language parallels rather than mimics nature. The cats inhabit white paper to avoid the distraction of other shapes and colours, and to reveal the wonderful equilibrium that is so apparent in silhouette.

Specific breed information comes from a variety of sources – mainly breeders, shows and my own library with references from many countries – but the underlying spirit of felinity in the paintings often derives from my own cats, and instinct. The inevitable dissection and reconstruction process that occurs gives the drawn icon a determination rarely matched by photography.

Roots

Although the cat has been domesticated for thousands of years it remains very similar to its wild ancestors. *Felis silvestris*, 'the forest wildcat', is a member of the cat family *Felidae*. The family includes thirty-seven species and, with the exception of the cheetah which has non-rectractile claws, they differ very little. All have flexible bodies, short jaws with specialized teeth, highly developed senses, large and well developed brains, digitigrade feet and retractile claws and a purr, although in the five big cats – lion, tiger, jaguar, leopard and snow leopard – it is a roar.

Felis silvestris must be considered the most highly successful carnivore in existence and it is distributed all over Europe, Africa and Asia. As with most widespread mammals the wild species evolved into a great many races, each adapted to local environment and climate. These include the European forest wildcat (*Felis silvestris silvestris*), the African wildcat (*Felis silvestris lybica*) and in the western Asiatic the Indian desert cat (*Felis silvestris ornata*). The Scottish wildcat is the northern 'cold climate' race with its heavily mackerel tabby striped coat, relatively heavy body and head, stocky limbs and small ears. The African wildcat is the southern 'warm climate' race, with finer limbs, larger ears, a smaller head and a coat that, while still mackerel

striped, shows more flecking. The Indian desert cat, also a 'warm climate' race, has a spotted tabby coat and slender body lines. The differences between the 'cold climate' and 'warm climate' races once led to a belief that they represented different species.

Domestication

In their original state the races of *Felis silvestris* tended to inhabit lowlands, swamps and forests. They began to associate with people when man first evolved from the hunter gatherer who roamed over large areas to become more settled and to develop the first agriculturally based societies. Cats scavenged around camp sites and villages and were at first tolerated and then, as their expertise in rodent control became apparent, encouraged.

Recent research suggests that the Egyptians may not have been the first to domesticate cats, as evidence of domestication about 9,000 years ago has been found in Jericho and about 4,000 years ago in the Indus valley. Recently the remains of a cat were identified in Cyprus and dated at about 7,000 years old. This last find is considered significant because there is no record of wild cats in Cyprus, and so the domesticated cats must have arrived there with the first human immigrants.

The Egyptians

Although there may have been isolated communities with domesticated cats elsewhere, the Ancient Egyptians were primarily responsible for introducing the domestic cat to the rest of the world. The Egyptians were interested in all animals and they kept a number of species in captivity. Pictures of cats have survived from the Middle Kingdom (2181–1567 BC) but these could be of wild animals. However there are many pictures of cats from the New Kingdom (1567–1085 BC) which clearly are domesticated, being portrayed sitting under chairs and hunting birds. These paintings make it clear that the Egyptian cat had descended from the local race of *Felis silvestris lybica*, sharing the shape, colour and pattern of its wild ancestor.

It was during the second millennium in ancient Egypt that the cat came to be regarded as a sacred animal. Herodotus, writing in about 450 BC, reported that

> Egypt, though it borders on Libya, is not a region abounding in wild animals. The animals that do exist in the country, whether domesticated or otherwise, are all regarded as sacred . . . . When a man has killed one of the sacred animals, if he did it with malice aforethought, he is punished with death, if unwittingly, he has to pay such a fine as the priests choose to impose.

He described as well how, when cats died, they were taken to the city of Bubastis where they were embalmed and buried in sacred repositories, and the bereaved owners shaved their eyebrows as a mark of respect. Not only cats but also mongooses, vultures, hawks and crocodiles were mummified. Cats were considered to be living representatives of the gods – the male cat representing the sun god Ra and the female cat the fertility goddess Bastet. (This goddess is also known as Bast and sometimes as Pasht, the latter name being a possible origin of the cat's name 'puss'.)

The Spread of the Cat: The Classical World

When Christianity came to Egypt and cats were no longer held to be sacred they began to be exchanged for other 'goods'. Gradually they spread throughout the Classical world. Prior to the coming of the cat the Greeks kept semi-domesticated weasels and skunks, and by comparison with these the cat would have been considered refined, clean and most importantly, not smelly. Another reason for their popularity was the spread of the brown rat and the house mouse. Records suggest that in Classical times the cat was valued more for its ability to control rats and mice than as a household pet.

While the exact route for the spread of the cat is not known it is likely that cats were taken to Persia by Egyptian armies attacking Pelusia, on the Egyptian border, in about 595 BC. By AD 500 the cat was well established there.

The Spread of the Cat: Islam

The most revered animal in Islam was once the horse, but when cats moved into the Arabian countries their popularity grew to equal, even to surpass, that of the horse. It is said that Muhammad owned a female cat named Muezza and that rather than disturb her when she was sleeping on his jellaba he cut off the section on which she was lying.

The Spread of the Cat: Europe and Asia

With the help of the Romans who established settlements throughout Europe and in Britain the cat spread rapidly. In 1974 the remains of fourteen cats were discovered at the Roman villa settlement of Tac in Hungary, and records of cat skeletons in the remains of Roman villas in Britain are well known. The commercial routes between Asia and Europe allowed for the spread of the cat into China before AD1000 where, in addition to being valued as a destroyer of mice, it was believed to symbolize peace, fortune and serenity. Even today divine powers are attributed to the cat in some Asiatic communities and it is believed that when a cat dies its soul speaks to Buddha in favour of the owner who still lives on earth. According to legend, the older and more hairless the cat, the more good fortune it will bring. But although the cat's ability to meditate was much admired by Buddhists it does not appear on the list of animals protected in the original canons of Buddhism. It is said that a cat fell asleep while on duty during the funeral ceremony of Buddha and that, as a result, the cat was excluded from the list.

Cats arrived in India at about the same time as in China and the feline divinity Sasht, the symbol of maternity, can be compared with the Egyptian goddess Bast. One rule of the Hindu religion is that one should always offer hospitality, or at least food, to a cat. From China cats moved into Japan and are said to have lived in the imperial palace of Kyoto from AD 999.

Cats and the Christian Church

St Patrick of Ireland in the fifth century and Pope Gregory Magro in the sixth century kept large numbers of cats, and cats are depicted in paintings of St Agatha and St Gertrude. Monasteries benefited from the cat's ability to hunt mice and some monastic orders, such as the Carthusians, actively bred cats. By Saxon times the cat was as familiar an animal in Britain as it is today. The famous Laws of Hywel Dda, the King of Wales, record in AD 945 that

The price of a cat is four pence. Her qualities are to see, to hear, to kill mice, to have her claws whole and to nurse, and not devour her kittens. If she be deficient in any of these qualities one third of her price must be returned.

Persecution

The cat was not much liked by the early Christian Church because of its heathen connections. In the middle of the thirteenth century, in response to the involvement of the cat in a revival of worship of the Norwegian goddess of fertility, the cat came to be seen as the embodiment of paganism and began to be actively persecuted. This irrational condemnation was easily accepted by fanatical people, who believed the cat to be a source of evil. It is never even mentioned in the Bible.

It was widely thought that witches could turn themselves into cats. During the reign of Mary Tudor of England cats were burned as embodiments of Protestantism, and in the reign of Elizabeth I they were burned as embodiments of the Catholic religion. Cats were especially tormented during Lent when it was a widespread practice to throw them into bonfires in order to burn out the devil. In France the festival of St John on 24 June remains infamous; in many town squares braziers were erected and fires lit upon which captured cats were thrown to burn among the hysterical cries of crowds who believed they were liberating themselves from the devil. These practices were endorsed by churchmen and kings alike; and as a result domestic cats were virtually extinct by 1400 when the bubonic plague, carried by rat fleas, struck Europe. There were insufficient cats to kill the rats and two-thirds of the European population died.

Even during the eighteenth century cats were persecuted and tortured in the course of baiting sports. Louis XIV did much to improve the lot of the cat when he prohibited the cat burning ceremonies, but only after the French Revolution were these practices of previous times seen to be cruel and the beliefs about cats discarded as pure superstition.

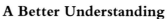

A Better Understanding

In the mid-1800s Louis Pasteur published details of his scientific discoveries and people began to understand that disease was transmitted rather than being inflicted as a punishment by God or the devil. It was realized that the cat provided a shining example of hygiene as it cleaned itself many times each day. The cat entered an era when it was particularly prized – especially if it had unusual characteristics such as lack of tail or long hair. Selective breeding to produce new varieties first started in the second half of the century as a direct result of urbanization, increased leisure time for people working in industry and a greater understanding of the processes of evolution. The keeping of pets became fashionable and many exotic varieties of bird, dog and cat were imported.

Towards the end of the century the name of Charles Cruft and the Cruft's dog show became famous and dog clubs were formed. Cat lovers, not to be outdone, followed suit and were championed by Harrison Weir, a fellow of the British Royal Horticultural Society and a writer and illustrator for the *Illustrated London News*, *The Field* and *The Graphic*. He was to become known worldwide as 'the father of the cat fancy'. He selected the Crystal Palace, built for the 1851 Great Exhibition in south London, as the venue for the first formal cat show, with different classes of cats being divided by shape, colour and build.

Although the earliest recorded cat show had taken place in 1598 the 1871 show was the first which conformed to specific rules and where cats were judged in accordance with particular specifications laid down by Harrison Weir.

The First Cat Shows

Harrison Weir separated the longhairs from the shorthairs and grouped them in different classes according to colour and shape. He drew up guides for judging and called these 'Standards of Excellence' or 'Standards of Points'. For the first time the number of marks awarded for the colour of coat or the shape of the body were laid down and judges very carefully followed the new rules. Harrison Weir later wrote:

The first cat show led up to the observation and kindly feeling for the domestic cat. Since then, throughout the length and breadth of the land, there have been Cat Shows, and much interest in them is taken by all classes of the community. Having before my mind many instances to show that Shows generate a love for cats I have never regretted planning the first Cat Show at the Crystal Palace.

A system to record the ancestry of cats was instituted and later, when cat clubs were established, each had its own register. The club stud book became its bible. Soon after the foundation of the British National Cat Club it was said that they had 2,000 cats on their breed registers.

The first cat shows in the USA took place in New England, but most people date the beginning of the American cat fancy from a show organized in 1895. Fired by enthusiasm after attending a cat show at the Crystal Palace, an Englishman, James Hyde, organized the show at the Madison Square Garden, New York. It promoted sufficient interest in the cat to lead to the formation of many cat clubs. The first and most important was the Beresford Cat Club, named in honour of Lady Marcus Beresford and under the presidency of Mrs Clinton Locke. Cat shows were soon held

throughout the USA and later in Australia, Canada, New Zealand, South Africa and Japan. In recent years successful cat shows have been held in Russia.

Books on Cats

In 1903 *The Book of the Cat*, edited by Frances Simpson, was to become the definitive work for all cat fanciers. She recruited specialists to write about the cat fancy in their own countries and others to write on particular breeds. She gave advice on show presentation. At that time, show cats were numbered and their number was written on a tally tied round the neck with ribbon. Frances Simpson advised:

Pink coloured ribbons are the most becoming to blue kittens until their eyes have changed, then orange or yellow will be found more suitable. It is a mistake to tie very broad ribbons round your cat's neck when sending them to a show. I should choose a colour to match the eyes, with half an inch to three quarters in width. Tie a neat bow and give a stitch in the centre. Don't leave too long ends. Orange is the most becoming colour for blue cats.

On pen furnishing she advised: 'If you are allowed to provide pussies with cushions at a show let the neck ribbon correspond in colour as this will have a better effect.'

In these early years cats and kittens were sent to shows unaccompanied. Kittens were exhibited from about eight weeks of age and few precautions on hygiene were observed. Small wonder that many cats died as a result of infection combined with the stresses of travel and exhibition at shows.

In the early days of the cat fancy women were not in the forefront as judges – the suffragettes had not yet commenced their campaign and women everywhere were primarily involved with domestic duties. Writing in 1900 the American Helen Winslow said:

A cat should be handled gently and kept as calm as possible during the judging. Women are naturally more gentle in their methods and more tender hearted. When my pets are entered in competition, may some wise, kind woman have the judging of them.

Soon after the publication of Helen Winslow's book women swamped the judging rings. Their 'tender hearts' won the day, and from that time until comparatively recently there were only a few men who achieved fame as judges.

The Pen Judging Show

The early cat shows were modelled on Cruft's, with the cats first displayed in pens on beds of straw and then paraded around a ring on lengths of ribbon. This practice was soon abandoned in favour of the system used in other small livestock fancies, where the animals were either judged in pens or taken to a table where the judge could assess them at close quarters. As the cat fancy grew the British exhibitors adopted a system where the cats are placed in pens and the judges move between the pens assessing the cats as they proceed. This system is still in use by the GCCF. To avoid confusion the classes of cats are penned together so that for example all blue Persians are in one section and all seal point Siamese are in another.

To assist the judges stewards are allocated whose responsibility is to lift the cats out of their pens, to handle them for the judge, to make certain that high standards of hygiene are observed and to keep a record of the judges' placings in order to avoid him or her committing the cardinal sin of 'cross judging'. Cross judging refers to a situation where two cats judged earlier in the day are judged again by the same judge but placed in different order. Each cat is judged several times and by several different judges. The important class, called 'the open', is the only one in which challenge certificates are awarded. The challenge certificates are much prized since their award by three different judges on three different occasions results in the cat being awarded a title such as champion.

Shows held by clubs affiliated to the GCCF are one-day affairs. Each cat's pen is furnished completely in white to avoid any possibility of the judges knowing the identity of the cat or its owner. Exhibitors are not allowed inside the judging area: results are posted in a special section of the show hall and short notes on the good and bad points of the winners are sent by the judge to a cat fancy magazine for later publication. In this type of show new breeds and varieties are entered in special 'assessment' classes where there is no competition but where each receives a written critique. Cats of recognized breeds compete for championships and grand championships with special premier titles for neuters. At the one show held each year by the GCCF itself, an additional set of titles – supreme champion and supreme premier – are offered.

The Ring Judging Show

When the American fanciers developed their show system they retained more of the characteristics of dog shows by moving the exhibits to the judge rather than making the judge move to the exhibits. Cats are exhibited to the general public in pens which occupy the main section of the hall, and pen decorations may be of any colour or style and with advertising matter on show if required. Additional pens, called holding pens, are placed behind the judges' table. Exhibitors take their cats to the pens behind the judge before the judging of each class and the judge then handles the cats herself. She has a clerk whose duty it is to announce the exhibit numbers required for the next class and to record the placings made by the judge. The stewards' only duty is to clean and sterilize the holding pens between each judging. All judging is done in public and judges are expected to provide a commentary while they work. Unlike the original British system, the American show allows for several rings with classes equivalent to the GCCF 'opens', so that an extremely good cat may become a champion in one show. Championships are gained by a complicated system of points rather than on the award of certificates.

The American system is used in all associations there and also in Canada

and Japan. It is now being tried alongside the European-style shows in France, Hungary and some other countries in Europe. In this system cats of new breeds compete in special 'new breed and colour' sections. Shows may be two, three or even four-day affairs and are held by affiliated clubs of the organizing body. The titles on offer are championships and grand championships, and additionally those qualifying for a title more than once can become double champions, triple champions and so on.

The International Show

In the European countries a slightly different style of show evolved as a mix of the other two. As in the USA cats are penned in the main hall where the public and the exhibitors can be with them all day and pens can be decorated in any colour or manner. Judges work from tables behind or alongside which are 'holding pens' to which the cats are taken by stewards. Judging is usually done in public and although the judge does not give a spoken commentary she is free to announce results and make verbal comments if she so wishes. Comments on all aspects of the cats are made on special report forms which are supplied to the exhibitors during the show.

In this style of show special classes are offered for cats of new breed or colour. Titles offered for winning cats are champion, international champion, grand international champion and champion of Europe. This last title is very hard to achieve as the winning cat must be assessed as ninety-eight per cent perfect on nine separate occasions. Neuter cats have their own series of titles. Shows may be one or two-day affairs, and the shows may be held either by the main organization or by a member club.

In Europe there are two main groups of fanciers holding this style of show: the Fédération Internationale Féline and the independent clubs of Europe. The European show system is also used in the CA of Britain which has now become a member of FIFe in order to take the British fancy into international circles.

The Making of Breed Type

The diversification of breeds from the stocky-bodied cold climate form and the slender-bodied warm climate form is a result of selective breeding from a variety of starting points. For example the extreme slender-bodied long-headed and large-eared Siamese of today is the result of selective breeding from the broader-chested, more stocky, shorter-headed cats with smaller ears which were exported from Thailand in the nineteenth century.

The domestic cat may be regarded as the middle of the natural range of cat types, with the European forest wildcat on one side and the African wildcat on the other. Selection in one direction for the extremes of heavy stocky type can be seen to have produced the Persian, while selection in the other direction for the extremes of slender, fine-boned type has produced the Oriental/Siamese. Between these two extremes lie the many other breed types. Those most closely resembling the domestic cat in build are the Chartreux, British, European and American Shorthairs.

The evolution of breeds with such different conformation has been possible because, with a few exceptions, the genes producing changes in conformation have a minimal individual effect. Such genes are known as polygenes. It is only when a large number of similar polygenes are inherited by any particular kitten that their effect will be expressed. Since every kitten inherits half its polygene complement from each parent it can easily be understood that matings between cats such as Persian and Siamese, at the extreme opposite ends of the range, will produce kittens very similar to domestics. But in the early days of selective breeding the barriers at the extreme ends of the range had not been pushed out to the absolute limits, so that the evolution of the show Persian from the cold climate type and the Siamese from the warm climate type took far longer than it took for say the silver Oriental to evolve from original crosses of Siamese with Persian. As photographs in books published over the last eighty years will testify, the process towards the present-day Persian must have taken something like eighty generations. In the Oriental programmes it took five.

Some polygenes tend to be inherited together, so that the simple blending effect

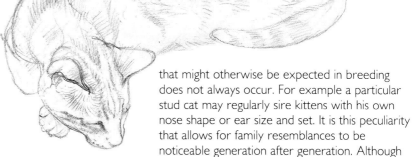

that might otherwise be expected in breeding does not always occur. For example a particular stud cat may regularly sire kittens with his own nose shape or ear size and set. It is this peculiarity that allows for family resemblances to be noticeable generation after generation. Although there are no actual 'nose genes' or 'ear set genes', the polygenes affecting these aspects have tended to stick together rather than freely intermix.

Unlike the dog the cat has an inbuilt resistance to drastic change in size – all breeds falling within a range of eight to fifteen pounds (4–7 kgs). This generally small size is probably part of the genotype of *Felis silvestris*, and reduction in size from the wild form is part of the process of domestication.

The Dangers of Over Selection

All modern breeds of cat are founded upon the basic cold climate and warm climate types and have been evolved by the manipulation of polygenes. Most breeds fall within the natural range of types, but some have been extended to the outermost limits. It is possible to breed cats beyond those limits, but they are likely to be abnormal. They may be unable to deliver kittens naturally, or to suckle naturally, and breathing difficulties and diseases of the ears and eyes may regularly occur.

Breeders' records suggest that the outer limits of viability in the cold climate type were reached with the Persian when it still had its nose leather appreciably below the lower level of the eyes, when its jaws were level or nearly level, when its rib cage occupied approximately half the length of its trunk and when there was a definite curve at the back of the head.

Although fewer problems are reported by breeders owning cats at the extremes of the warm climate type, the reduced fertility and viability and the shortened lives of many of the extremely long-headed, narrow-bodied Siamese suggests that the outer limits have also been reached here; although some problems in this breed may also result from inbreeding.

Both British associations have drawn up lists of characteristics they consider to be harmful to cats and have instructed their judges to disqualify or mark down cats with these defects. They also advise breeders to discontinue breeding with cats that regularly produce defective kittens and avoid inbreeding with lines that have produced them. Remedial action will take time, as selection towards the more natural cat must be practised and this will take just as long as it did for selection to be practised in the opposite direction. If remedial action is not taken the breeds at the outer limits of the natural cat range will be forced to live in pain and discomfort and man will have returned to the dark ages when he tortured cats by other means.

Structural Differences

In addition to the many breeds produced as a result of selective breeding there are several breeds which have a structural difference which is inherited separately. Breeds in this category include the Manx, whose taillessness results from the presence of a dominant gene; the Scottish Fold, whose little folded ears result from the presence of a dominant gene; the Japanese Bobtail whose tiny curly/kinked tail results from a recessive, or perhaps incompletely recessive, gene; the American Curl, whose extended outward curling ears result from a dominant gene. Recently reports have been made on a bobtailed cat which is said to result from a mutant gene occurring in Ragdolls. The variety is provisionally named American Bobtail but little is known of its genetics. Cats with additional toes are sometimes bred as a result of the dominant gene for polydactylism but all cat show organizations disqualify such exhibits.

Coat Types

In addition to the variations in conformation which have been achieved by selective breeding there are many variations in the type and quality of coat. Some cats have long hair; some cats have short hair; some cats have wavy hair; some cats have wire hair; and some cats have virtually no hair at all. The long outer coat and dense woolly undercoat of the Persian can be regarded as one extreme, while a short, flat-lying coat devoid of anything but minimal undercoat represents the other extreme. Both characteristics are under the control of genes for coat length. The gene for short hair is dominant over that for long hair, so that if a cat has one or two genes for short hair it will have short hair. If it has two genes for longhair it will have long hair. There are other differences in the degree of length, the woolliness or silkiness of hair and the degree of undercoat and these, like body shape, are controlled by polygenes.

Other coat types are those of rex waviness (see pages 118–122), and wirehair (see page 26). There is also a cat, the Sphynx (see page 80), which has hair only on the ears, paws and tail.

Colours and Patterns

There are a host of colours and patterns and while some are considered acceptable in certain breeds others are not. As breeders become more expert in the detection of colour differences, different varieties of colour are classified and, in some cases, new colour varieties are accepted for showing. This was the process involved when the chocolate point Siamese was granted recognition after years of being considered as a 'poor' seal point. Three more new colours are caramel, apricot and indigo – respectively a chalky coloured taupe, the colour of apricot skins and a very deep blue. All these colours occur in Siamese, Orientals and Burmese.

The vast majority of coat varieties result from the re-combination

of well known colour and pattern genes and nearly all of them are inherited in a simple dominant or recessive fashion. Most breed clubs publish charts to help their members breed for the colours of their choice. Confusingly colours are often known by different names in different breeds. For example the auburn colour described in the Turkish Van is red in other breeds and the sorrel of the Abyssinian is cinnamon in the Oriental Shorthair. Even more confusingly the CFA still refers to the sorrel Abyssinian as red and the GCCF describes the ruddy Abyssinian as 'usual'.

Different associations have different colour names for tabbies – the tabby cat with brown agouti ground and black tabby pattern is known as brown tabby in the GCCF whereas in FIFe and most other associations it is black tabby. There are historical reasons for this anomaly as the 'browns' were the only colour considered when cat varieties were first classified, blue tabbies, with blue tabby pattern and bluish beige ground colour being consigned to the Any Other Colour classes. Newer associations are able to be more logical and the usual procedure today is to name a tabby colour by the colour of the pattern.

Tortoiseshell and tortoiseshell and white cats have a variety of names. The correct full name is tortoiseshell but it is conventional to shorten this to tortie and to describe cats with a combination of tabby and tortie markings as torbie. However some associations describe torbies as patched tabbies or use the full name of tortoiseshell tabby. In the USA tortie and whites are often known as 'calicos' as their blotches of colour on white are reminiscent of the patterned calicos of the famous East India company in the nineteenth century.

The Skin and Coat

The appearance of a cat's coat gives a good indication of the state of its health, although sometimes even healthy cats will have poor quality coats as a result of the 'busy owner syndrome'. This is more likely to occur in longhair breeds for whom care and grooming is essential. If you leave the main responsibility for grooming with your cat the result will be an unhappy cat, suffering from digestive disturbances due to the presence of swallowed hair in the gut (hairball) and from knots of hair close to the skin which

makes every movement painful. Grooming improves the coat not only by separating hairs so that they fall separately and are free of knots but also by stimulating circulation to the skin, thus improving the coat itself.

Three main factors are involved in a healthy coat: nutrition, freedom from internal and external parasites and heredity. For optimum coat condition the cat's diet must contain a balanced mix of all essential proteins, amino acids, essential fatty acids and vitamins, as hair is ninety-five per cent protein and also contains large amounts of sulphur and amino acids.

Research has shown that at certain times of the year up to thirty per cent of the cat's daily protein requirement may be used to supply the skin and coat. In its wild state the cat lived on small mammals and birds, consuming all or nearly all of the bodies in order to obtain an adequate diet. Its body had adapted to a carnivorous diet over millions of years before the cat was first domesticated comparatively recently. So it is not surprising that cats living on a diet which mimics that of the wildcat look and do better than those fed on table scraps or mixed meat/fish/cereal diets without correct vitamin and mineral supplementation. Although many of the older breeders had their favourite recipes for feeding cats, the greater understanding of the cat's nutritional requirements and palate brought about by recent research in the pet food industry has served the cat well. Apart from certain exceptions, such as that of many Oriental type cats who cannot tolerate certain canned products including cow's milk derivatives, the majority of cats do best on the premium quality commercial foods – dry and canned – and the difference in their coats makes the extra cost well worthwhile.

Freedom from parasites is the right of all cats. While wildcats may have been infested with both worms and fleas, infestation would probably not have been heavy because they did not live in confined spaces or in close proximity to others of their kind and they were well adapted to cope. The pedigree cat has no such chance as he must share litter trays with others,

must sleep and live in shared quarters and spend his life in close proximity with other cats. The free-roaming domestic cat fares little better, as he has lost the tolerance that his wild ancestors had naturally acquired. Parasites can kill. The history of the Siamese reveals that kitten losses in the early days of the breed were severe and only when it was nearly too late did breeders realize that the problem was worm infestation. Preparations for the control of worms in cats and kittens are on general sale in pet shops and at cat shows. They are also available from all veterinary surgeons, who can give advice on frequency and methods of treatment. A cat carrying a burden of worms cannot be well nourished. Inadequate nutrition is reflected in the condition of the skin and coat very quickly – whether it results from the owner's failure to provide an adequate diet or failure to make sure that the cat, rather than its worms, gets the nourishment. The coat may become dry, brittle and dull, there may be prolonged periods of shedding, there may be areas of hairlessness, the skin may become excessively pigmented or the hair may actually lose pigment. Finally the skin may become thickened.

Parasites such as fleas or ticks aggravate the cat and cause itching. In some cats the itching/scratching cycle may become so prolonged that a generalized inflammation results and the help of a veterinary surgeon is required. Fleas can be easily detected by the presence of tiny black specks in the coat, usually around the root of the tail. If you find such specks, try dropping them into water. If they are reddish coloured when wet, like blood, you can be certain that your cat has fleas and flea control preparation is urgently required.

Providing that you ensure that your cat is free from parasites and has an adequate diet his coat should be in generally good condition. The normal skin and coat accumulates debris such as oil from glands in the skin, sloughed skin cells and dirt. Grooming is necessary in order to remove these. Some breeds require more owner-grooming than others, and grooming procedures are described more fully in the sections preceding each breed group. In general it can be said that a regular grooming schedule is vitally important.

Grooming Routines

The grooming undertaken by the cat itself is often adequate for some shorthair breeds but if the cat is old, or there is a problem such as a waxy or brown gritty exudate in the ears, the help of the owner will be required. Longhair cats, whether pedigree or non-pedigree, always require the owner's attention. If cats are to be exhibited there are specific requirements that must be complied with and these vary slightly in each breed or breed group. Shampoos and cleansing agents are often used before shows but care must be taken over their selection. A good shampoo should remove excess oil, dirt and debris, cleanse and separate the hairs and leave the coat shiny and easy to comb. There must be no residue in the coat and the shampoo must not remove too much oil, irritate the eyes or contain toxins that may be absorbed through the skin to make the cat ill. A variety of specialist cat shampoos are available: the mildest are those made from coconut or palm oils.

Grooming involves giving attention to the ears, teeth, claws and coat and benefits the cat by improving its sense of well-being. The ears should be carefully checked and cleaned. Any wax can be wiped away with a dry cotton bud in shorthairs and a piece of cotton wool moistened with a water and shampoo mix in longhairs. The long ear furnishings in Persians sometimes become sticky with wax. It is important to avoid water trickling down inside the ears.

The gums should be regularly checked for signs of inflammation and the teeth should be carefully examined. Many cats lose some of the tiny teeth at the front of the mouth at a comparatively early age but provided that the remaining teeth are in good condition no action need be taken by the owner. If there is evidence of excess tartar or

groomed and details are given in the preface to each breed group. However a bran bath is sometimes indicated for all cats and can be undertaken by warming about 100–150 g of bran on a baking tray in a warm oven and then massaging the warm bran through the cat's coat. Ideally the cat should then be wrapped in warm towels for about ten minutes and then combed and brushed to remove the bran and the dirt, scurf and loose hairs. The following day the combing and brushing routine should be repeated.

During grooming the skin should be checked for scratches, scabs or patches of bare skin. If such lesions are present on a cat entered in a show their presence may result in a ban on entry. Whether the cat is a show goer or not, any lesions should be taken seriously. It is often wise to get unexplained lesions checked by a veterinary surgeon.

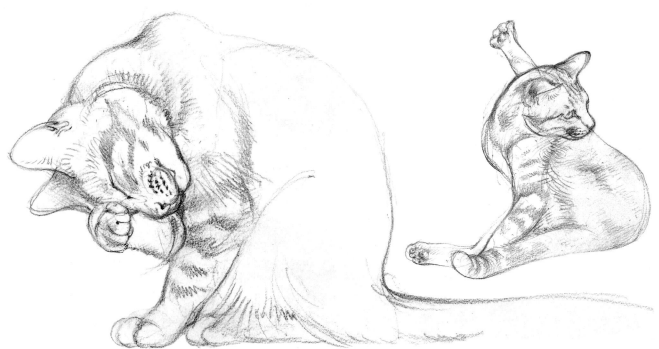

General Care

For a cat to be healthy and live a life as near as possible to the ideal it needs adequate nutrition, the provision of clean water at all times, the provision of a litter box that is regularly cleaned and changed and an environment where there is human company and ample opportunity for exercise and sufficient stimulation to keep it happy and well balanced. If it is a longhaired cat the owner must schedule time for special grooming sessions.

On no account should cats be turned out to roam the streets or countryside at night. Although in their original wild state they were night hunters they were completely adapted to an outdoor life. The domesticated cat is not so suited to the rigours of climate: he lives a softer, longer life and it is cruel and unthinking to pamper a cat in a centrally-heated house or flat or

infection in the mouth a visit to the veterinary surgeon is indicated.

The claws should be checked to make sure that none is broken or splintered and to ensure that the area around each claw and between the paw pads is clean and free from infection or inflammation. The claws themselves can be tipped by the use of nail clippers. The cat's foot is turned so that the clippers cut cleanly across the flattened sides of the claw and do not crush it downwards, causing it to splinter. Only the tips of the claws should be removed. No cat should be de-clawed as to do so would restrict its ability to climb or to protect itself. In Britain the CA requires that all cats exhibited at shows have the tips of their claws removed.

The methods of grooming the coat vary with the type of cat to be

before a fire during the day and then to throw him out to cope with the weather conditions in the outside world at night. Pet cats living in the home have a right to night-time accommodation in a warm position and a litter box within easy access. The advances made in the manufacture of cat litters over the last two decades make it unnecessary for any human to object to a cat litter box on grounds of smell. With modern litters and boxes there will be a smell only if the owner fails to empty them regularly.

There are other reasons why cats can no longer roam as freely as they once did and although some of these apply also to domestic pets they are of extreme importance to breeders and owners of unneutered pedigree cats. Cats roaming gardens and streets risk being attacked by cat-haters,

who are recorded as practising unspeakable cruelties. They also risk being run over, killed by dogs, or stolen. Exposure to other cats combined with chill and stress may result in respiratory disease (cat flu); feline leukaemia, feline infectious enteritis and several other cat diseases including the feline Aids virus known to be particularly prevalent in domestic cats. Because of these dangers most owners of pedigree cats organize feline exercise and sunning areas in their own gardens or on their own balconies protected from other cats, cars, dogs and humans.

Choosing a Cat

There are several golden rules which you should apply when choosing a cat or kitten. It is sensible to research the differences between breeds, to decide which breed is most likely to be happy with your home, and to be certain that you definitely want a pedigree cat. With a few exceptions the non-pedigree domestic cats can be just as loving and amusing as their pedigree counterparts. On the other hand they cost as much to care for as the pedigree cats.

In general cat behaviour and personality are not drastically affected by cruelty or lack of care in a bad home so that a cat from a shelter is likely to be a very successful family pet if given a second chance in life. Although

kittens are always in great demand, a cat will already have gone through all the possible problems of kittenhood and, if you obtain it from a reputable shelter, will be spayed (neutered) thus avoiding the problem of an unexpected and unwanted litter of kittens followed by an operation to avoid the complication in future.

It is important to choose a well-run cat shelter where cats are kept in hygienic conditions and well cared for. The cat should look bright and alert, its eyes should be clean and without any trace of discharge and it should be free of any matter around the anus or in the ears. Its coat should be free of fleas and flea dirt.

Another good way to obtain a domestic cat is to book a kitten from a litter owned by a friend or neighbour. Although the newcomer will be a kitten and not a full-grown cat you should observe the same precautions in selection. It would be foolish to take a kitten with sore or runny eyes or evidence of diarrhoea.

Pedigree kittens are advertised in magazines printed especially for the cat fancy. Alternatively you can contact one of the cat fancy organizations for details of clubs and breeders. The main bodies such as TICA, FIFe and GCCF keep lists of member clubs and the officials of member clubs keep lists of breeders in their membership. It is never wise to buy a pedigree kitten from any person other than its breeder. He or she will know the complete history of the kitten from the day it was born, its inoculations against Feline Infectious Enteritis and cat flu will have been completed and the pedigree details and registration documents will be available. If you plan to show the kitten or breed from it the provision of the pedigree and registration documents is vital, in fact part of the price you pay for the kitten is for its pedigree and registration. Some associations, such as the GCCF, register kittens by issuing small certificate slips, and the breeder prepares the pedigree by hand. Others, like the CA in Britain and the associations of FIFe, have always issued official pedigrees. Although in these associations the breeder may still provide a hand-written copy, that official pedigree is the one included in the price of the kitten. The breeder also supplies details of a recommended diet.

The Shorthair Group

From a tiny child to the present, the love of nature has been my chief delight; animals and birds have not only been my objects of study, but of deep and absorbing interest. I have noted their habits, watched their ways and found lasting pleasure in their companionship. This love of animal life and nature, with all its moods and phases, has grown with me from childhood to manhood, and is not the least enjoyable part of my old age. Among animals possibly the most perfect, and certainly the most domestic, is the Cat.

The first shows were almost entirely given over to shorthairs, and until the National Cat Club took over the running of the Crystal Palace shows in

The Shorthair group includes all of the shorthair breeds with the heavier body type inherited by European domestic cats from the cold climate form of wildcat. For convenience the group can be classified into four sub-groups. The first consists of breeds primarily evolved by natural selection from the basic domestic cat. This includes the American Shorthair, the British Shorthair, the Chartreux and the European Shorthair. The second sub-group comprises breeds evolved as a result of gene mutation; these are the American Curl, the American Wirehair, the Manx and the Scottish Fold. The third sub-group is one of contrived breeds – cats designed by man from the combination of characteristics already present in other breeds. This includes the Exotic Shorthair and the Californian Spangled Cat. The last group at present includes one breed only – a large shorthaired cat with markings similar to those of the classic tabby. This little-known breed, called Sokoke, is currently being developed in Denmark from basic stock imported from Africa.

Within the American/British/Chartreux/European complex there are subtle differences in coat texture, quite major differences in coat colour and pattern and sufficient difference in conformation to make differentiation of the four different breeds quite easy. The origin of the American and European from the domestic breeds in each continent is evident to the eye.

It was Harrison Weir's love of the shorthair cat that led to the establishment of the cat fancy. In presenting his first official breed standards he wrote:

The notes and illustrations of and respecting the Cat are the outcome of over fifty years' careful study, thoughtful, heedful observation, much research, and not unprofitable attention to the facts and fancies of others.

1896 very little attention was paid to longhairs. The first cat show catalogues contained the names of many important shorthairs: silver tabbies seemed to be the most popular and one of them, named Champion Jiminy, was said to be worth £1,000. There seems to have been a good deal of confusion between British Blues and the contemporary Russian Blues. In fact one exhibitor wrote to *Fur and Feather* complaining that 'The last time I showed my Russian was in a class supposedly for Russians only. She was, however, beaten by a round-headed British Blue.'

Black and whites did better because there was no confusion over their standards and one of the most beautiful was Tyneside Lily. Her judges commented on her beautiful white coat and exquisite type and one of them added: 'This cat retains the racy workmanlike character of the true British-bred cat.' Some of the tortoiseshells were outstanding, particularly a female with the unusual name of Samson.

The British Shorthair is now regarded as the snob breed of the shorthairs, having forgotten its humble beginnings when breeders used to mate out to Persian every fifth generation. By this means the British acquired a rounder head, smaller ears, thicker limbs and shorter body. However the practice had unfortunate repercussions in the USA, where registries classified the British with the Exotic Shorthair purely because of its Persian connections. This decision has now been reversed and the British Shorthair is doing well as a legal immigrant.

The habit of the British GCCF of classifying every colour variety of British Shorthair as a separate breed has caused much confusion among novice breeders. It has also allowed different colour varieties to develop at different rates. As a result some varieties have larger ears, longer muzzles or legs than others. The many colours bred are those inherited from farm cats with the addition, in some registries, of chocolate and lilac. One of the oldest varieties is the black – considered by the British to be good luck cats despite the fact that black cats were once regarded as the companions of devils and witches. Black British Shorthair kittens often show faint tabby markings in their coats and these may not totally disappear until the kitten is nearly adult. Whites are bred with orange eyes, blue eyes or one of each, and often show a little smudge of coloured hairs on the head during kittenhood. This coloured smudge will be made up from hairs of the basic genetic colour masked by the white coat.

Blue-creams were recognized in Britain more recently but remain a fairly rare variety because, as blue tortoiseshells, they normally occur only if female. Any hint of tabby markings in the coat of a blue cream is a bad fault at shows and so breeders usually avoid mating females of this variety to tabby males. As in torties an elongated cream (red in torties) mark, known as a blaze, is often present in the centre of the forehead and cats with this mark are particularly favoured. When tortie markings of any colour are combined with white the patches of colour become larger and more clear-cut.

Manx were always popular and were exhibited in great numbers although many judges considered absence of tail to be the only criterion and completely ignored the standards laid down by Harrison Weir. Frances Simpson, who was a Persian fanatic, saw nothing beautiful about the Manx and described them as 'grotesque and of unfinished appearance but very sporting cats and great favourites with the sterner sex'. A consistent show winner, much admired by his judges, was Champion Finchey Boy.

The American Shorthair evolved naturally from domestic cats with its origins among the cats accompanying the Pilgrim Fathers, and the breed is much the same today as it was in its original form. Because of this the early USA cat fanciers tended to take it for granted and to choose their show cats from other, more exotic breeds. The breed only gained its rightful place in USA show halls in 1966. The 1988 winner of the title Best Premier in the CFA was Grand Premier and Grand Champion NW Briarson Babette of Midnite, a brown patched tabby bred by Sheree Dachman and Brian Pearson and owned by Lucia Pozzi.

The European Shorthair has a similar history to its American cousin. Evolved naturally from house and street cats, the exhibition Domestic Shorthairs in Europe were at first undervalued and the only shorthair breeds considered to be of any value were the British and the Exotic. Its upgrading to its present position is almost entirely due to the forward-thinking Finnish cat fanciers, who campaigned hard for its inclusion in show classification as the native shorthair breed of Europe.

The Chartreux, although similar in many respects to the American, British and European Shorthairs, has a totally different ear set and coat texture and is of generally heavier build. It was always regarded as a native breed of France (see page 30), although in the years when European shows were dominated by the British Shorthair it came to be considered simply as a French variation of that breed. In books on cats published in Britain the word Chartreux was mentioned only as an alternative name for British Blue; one British breeder imported a Chartreux and was able to register its progeny as full British Shorthair as recently as the 1960s. However the French still regarded the breed as their own, and the writer Colette enhanced the reputation of the Chartreux by choosing one as her pet. The Chartreux is now establishing itself in the USA and is doing well throughout Europe. In Cologne, Germany, lives the famous Champion of Europe, Pandur's Attila. Born in 1979 and bred by K. Bandurski, he is owned by Renate Schmidt. His massive type has won him admirers in many countries and he is affectionately known as 'Attila the Hun'.

The American Curl and the American Wirehair have their origin in the American domestic cat. American breeders, always keen to breed anything unusual, were quick to spot the potential of cats with curly ears. The shorthair Curl is simply another coat length variety of the American Curl (see page 22). The American Wirehair also has a solid background of American domestic cats and its owners plan to keep it that way.

The Scottish Fold had its origins in domestic cats in Scotland and the first outcrosses were made to British Shorthairs. When the breed registers were closed by the British GCCF on grounds that the breed might have a propensity towards infestation with ear mites it emigrated to the USA where it is now firmly established (and has clean ears!) It is making its mark in Australia and in several countries of Europe and is now a national championship breed in the British CA.

One of the contrived breeds of the group is the Exotic Shorthair, first recognized when it was divided from the American Shorthair. It is a magnificent breed which although originating in the USA has been bred with great success in Europe. One of the most famous European Exotics of all time is Champion of Europe Ubi Bene Ibi El Kahena (known to his friends as Benni). A magnificent blue, he was bred in Switzerland by Marga Speck and now resides in the Netherlands with Ari Groenevegen. Benni travelled to New York in 1986 to do battle with the greats of his breed in their native land. He won, his name went up in lights in the main arena of the Madison Square Garden, his photograph was flashed across the USA and his European fan club were beside themselves with delight.

The Californian Spangled Cat is not recognized by any association although its striking appearance and its unusual history justify its inclusion in the group. It has the distinction of being the only breed of cat to be launched by the famous Nieman-Marcus Christmas catalogue. It was contrived by a Californian screen writer, Paul Casey, to evolve as a wild-looking cat of domestic origin. Its ancestral breeds include a traditional Siamese, an Angora-type silver tabby, a spotted Manx, a domestic/Abyssinian cross breed and a domestic shorthair from Malaysia. The result was named the Californian Spangled because its spotted coat is similar to the spangled pattern of birds and because it evolved in California.

Grooming cats of the shorthair group is relatively simple, involving brushing to stimulate circulation and to remove dust and loose hair. Show preparation more often involves a bran bath than a wet shampoo which might over-soften the coat texture.

American Curl Shorthair

Name
Named because of its curled ears.

Origins
In June 1981 two young kittens arrived, uninvited, to stay with Joe and Grace Ruga of Lakewood, California. Both were female and longhaired, one black and the other black and white. Both had unusual ears, with the cartilage curled backwards. The black and white kitten resumed her travels after only a week but the other adopted the Rugas and stayed on to become Joe's 'shoulder cat'.

The Rugas named the kitten Shulasmith. They noticed her unusual ears but considered it nothing more than an oddity until, among the four kittens in her first litter born on 12 December 1981, were two with curly ears. Grace gave one of the kittens, a female long-haired tabby curl, to her sister Esther Brimlow, who lived in Orange, California. The kitten was named Mercedes and in due course she produced a litter which included more kittens with curled ears.

It was when Nancy Kiester, owner of a local meat market, was making a delivery to the Brimlow's home that she chanced to see Mercedes and her kittens. She bought two – a longhair brown mackerel tabby female and a shorthair brown spotted tabby male, and named them Princess Leah and Master Luke. Soon after this Nancy Kiester noticed an article in her local paper on the origin of the Scottish Fold. She realized the similarity between the two types of cat and was further inspired by reading the section on the possible breeds of the future in *The Book of the Cat*. She got in touch with the Rugas and on 23 October 1983 they got together and entered Shulasmith, Master Luke and Princess Leah in the non-competitive section of the Riata Cat Club Show at Palm Springs, California.

They took advice from Jean Grimm, a Scottish Fold breeder in the CFA, on the compilation of a breed standard, naming the original longhairs American Curl and the shorthairs American Curl Shorthairs. They set about showing their cats in associations including TICA, ACA, ACFA, CFA, UCF and CFF. The Rugas had registered a cattery name of Curlnique and the American Curl had arrived.

Conformation
A medium-size breed with a moderately long, semi-foreign-type body and medium-thick legs, the Curl has a fairly long tail. Its head shows a moderate length of muzzle, known as a modified wedge, slightly longer than wide. The main characteristic is the ears which are moderately large, wide at the base, rounded at the tips but with the tips curled back and pointing towards, but not touching, the centre of the back of the skull.

Coat
Short and soft, lying flat but not close-lying, with a minimal undercoat.

Colours
All colours accepted.

Patterns
All coat patterns accepted, including the Siamese.

Eyes
Any colour, not necessarily in keeping with coat colour, although colour pointed cats must have blue eyes.

Personality
Bold, active yet very tolerant and loving.

Voice
Moderate and variable as in the domestic cat.

Kittens
Born with apparently normal ears but they begin to curl four to seven days after birth. From that time ears remain tightly curled up to about the seventh week but then begin gradually to unfurl. By the time kittens are six months old the degree of curl is set for life.

Show Status
Recognized for championship competition by TICA. Accepted for registration by ACA, ACFA, CFA and CFF; as medallist breed by the CA of Britain 1986; recognized as a championship breed by the independent clubs of Europe. Shown in USA, Canada, Japan and some countries in Europe.

Breeding
Pedigrees may include unregistered domestic cats.

Black mackerel tabby American Curl Shorthair

American Shorthair

Name
Named after the country of its evolution from domestic cats. In the very early years of the breed it was known simply as Shorthair; then Domestic Shorthair until 1965.

Origins
Originating from the domestic cats owned by the first settlers from Britain and later from other European countries, the American Shorthair was allowed to breed without interference from man and thus its basic characteristics were evolved by natural rather than by artificial selection. When the first cat show was held in 1895 and the Beresford Cat Club was formed in 1899 the American Shorthair was not considered worthy of a place alongside the more exotic Persians, Abyssinians and Siamese, and for many years it was completely ignored. Only when the first cat show was held at the Madison Square Garden in New York did the breed make its debut as a show cat under the name of Shorthair. A standard for judging was compiled and the registers were opened to cats of unknown parentage. As a result American cat lovers had an opportunity to assess their cats in relation to the standard. If they were considered to 'fit' they could register and show them as Shorthairs. The first Shorthair to be registered was a cat imported from Great Britain in about 1900, named Belle of Bradford. Unusually for a cat named Belle he was a male – with a coat described as 'orange tabby'. He was imported by Jane Cathcart and bred by a Mr Kuhnel. Jane Cathcart subsequently imported a second Shorthair – this time a silver tabby male bred by Mrs Collingwood and named Pretty Correct. Then, in 1904, Jane Cathcart registered the first true American Shorthair. He was born in 1904 and named Buster Brown. He had a black smoke coat and his ancestry was of unknown domestic cats of America. Many more such cats were registered as breeders followed the example of Jane Cathcart and realized the attractiveness of the cats sitting on their own doorsteps.

However, the breed was not generally popular until 1964 when a Domestic Shorthair male beat off competition from other breeds to become Kitten of the Year. In 1965 Grand Champion Shawnee Trademark owned by Nikki Shuttleworth of Kentucky was named Cat of the Year, and soon the title Domestic Shorthair was dropped in favour of the designation American Shorthair.

Once the breed was established breeders set about outcrossing to other breeds such as Burmese, to obtain more stockiness and a rounder head, and to Persian, to obtain larger heads and more substance overall. The result was that the American Shorthair began to change towards the breed now known as Exotic Shorthair. Just in time the American cat fancy authorities realized that they were in danger of losing their native shorthair breed, and in 1966 Jane Martinke of Delaware proposed that separate classes be offered for the true American Shorthair and the short-haired Persian look-alikes. The latter group were named Exotic Shorthair and breeders of the former group renewed their efforts to preserve the natural characteristics of the true American Shorthair.

Conformation
A medium to large cat with a comparatively large head, slightly longer than wide and with a squarish muzzle and firm chin. The body is muscular with a slightly longer body than in British Shorthair and with strong, well-muscled legs culminating in large, well-rounded paws and a moderately long tail.

Coat
Short, very thick and even and fairly harsh in texture.

Colours
White; black; blue; red; cream; brown tabby (black tabby); blue tabby; red tabby; cream tabby; black silver tabby; black smoke; blue smoke; cameo smoke; black tortie smoke; black shaded silver; chinchilla; shell cameo; shaded cameo; black tortie; blue cream; calico (black tortie/white); dilute calico (blue tortie/white); van calico (van tortie/white); van blue cream/white; brown patched tabby (torbie); blue patched tabby (torbie).

Patterns
Solid; classic (blotched) tabby; mackerel tabby; spotted tabby; shaded; chinchilla (tipped); smoke; tortie; calico (tortie and white); van; van calico (van tortie and white); patched tabby (torbie).

Eyes
Blue, brilliant gold or one blue and one brilliant gold in whites. Brilliant gold in all other colours except chinchilla and shaded silver when it is green or blue-green, and silver tabby when it is green or hazel.

Variation
Very little indeed.

Personality
Described by its breeders as an unassuming cat with a four-square approach to life.

Voice
Moderately loud. Said to have a cry that is neither demanding nor meek.

Kittens
Kittens develop at about the same speed as kittens of the domestic cats from which the breed evolved.

Show Status
A championship breed in the USA, Canada, and Japan from the 1930s. Granted medallist status in Britain in 1986.

Breeding
Only American Shorthairs allowed in pedigrees in most associations.

Red classic tabby American Shorthair

American Wirehair

Name
The name describes its coat type and country of origin.

Origins
The breed's characteristic wirehair coat occurred as a result of mutation in 1966. A red and white male kitten was born on a farm in the New York area. His owner contacted Mrs William O'Shea, who bred a rex at her Hi-Fi cattery. Mrs O'Shea purchased the kitten and his normal-coated litter sister and named them Council Rock Farm Adam of Hi-Fi and Tip-Toe of Hi-Fi. Adam was red and white and Tip-Toe was reputed to be brown tabby and white, although breeding records indicate that she was actually brown patched tabby (torbie) and white. Coat samples were sent to Britain for investigation. It was confirmed that the wirehair is different from all other coat types in cats and agreed that it would be called 'Wirehair'. Although she wisely purchased two kittens in order to obtain more wirehairs, even if the gene involved was recessive, Mrs O'Shea and her colleagues subsequently established that it was dominant: so that the birth of two more wirehairs in a litter of four produced by Adam and Tip-Toe was entirely due to their sire. Adam was subsequently mated to an unrelated blue-eyed white shorthair and again two wirehairs and two normal-coated kittens were born. The next mating was of a red and white female from Adam and Tip-Toe. She was put to her sire and in due course she produced two red and white wirehair kittens.

It was at this point that other cat fanciers became interested and over the next few years kittens were acquired by Mr and Mrs William Beck of Maryland, Robert Bradford of Illinois and Dr Rosamunde Stevens Peltze of the Katzenreich cattery in Georgia. Hi-Fi's Amy of Katzenreich lived an extremely long, productive life and was still alive in 1978. After a period of further selective breeding Anne Bickman of the Chinquapin cattery in Georgia and Charles Hutto, also of Georgia, took up the breed. At this point kittens were sent to Germany to Elkhe Frehse and to Canada to Conway Lewis. In May 1969 Katzenreich's Barberry Ellen was born in a litter by Adam from Amy and later proved to be the first homozygous, or true-breeding, American Wirehair.

The breed caused a minor sensation when it was first shown because of its extraordinary coat. By 1985 the yearly total of wirehair registrations was nearing fifty and the breed, although still rare, was well established.

Conformation
Identical to the American Shorthair with good width of chest, a strong muscular body, firm limbs, rounded paws and a medium-length tail. Head just as in the American Shorthair. Although the basic conformation is the same as the Shorthair, the Wirehair appears to be thinner and rangier.

Coat
The coat is springy and of medium length with individual hairs crimped, hooked or bent. The density of the coat sometimes leads to ringlet formations rather than waves.

Colours
White; black; blue; red; cream; black silver; cameo; black tortie; blue cream; brown (black); tabby; blue tabby; patched tabby (torbie); blue patched tabby (torbie); also other colours under the heading 'other Wirehair colours' except chocolate, lavender (lilac), Siamese pattern or those colours/patterns with white.

Patterns
Solid; chinchilla (tipped silver); shaded silver; shell cameo; shaded cameo; smoke; classic (blotched) tabby; mackerel tabby; tortoiseshell; bi-colour; van bi-colour; calico (tortie and white); van calico (van tortie and white); patched tabby (tortie).

Eyes
Blue, brilliant gold or one eye each of blue and brilliant gold in whites; brilliant gold in most other colours except chinchilla or shaded silver when it is blue-green or green, and silver tabby when it is green or hazel.

Personality
Zany but sweet-tempered.

Voice
Moderate, although some cats are noisier than others.

Kittens
Kittens are born with wiry coats although the full effect is not apparent until the kitten is several months old.

Show Status
Recognized as a championship breed by all associations in the USA. Also shown in Canada, Japan and Germany.

Breeding
Only American Wirehairs and American Shorthairs are allowed in pedigrees.

Blue classic tabby American Wirehair

British Shorthair

Name
Registered as Exotic Shorthair in the USA until recently.

Origins
First recorded as a show cat when the artist Harrison Weir compiled 'points of excellence' for the English cat – a method of allocating marks out of 100 when judging. He organized the first cat show in Britain in 1871, which proved enormously popular. In 1887 the National Cat Club was founded with Harrison Weir as its first President and by the end of the century the English or British cats were recognized in a variety of colours. Registers of pedigrees were kept to so that the term pedigree cat became synonymous with show cat. In 1876 Dr Gordon Staples published *The Domestic Cat* and described the British Shorthair in great detail. Among the most famous champions at the turn of the century were Mr R. J. Hughes' Amber Queen, black with amber eyes; Xenophon, a brown tabby owned by Lady Decies; and the brown tabby Ballochmyle Brown Bump, owned by Lady Alexander. Silver tabbies were highly prized and in 1870 it is recorded that they were priced at around fifty pounds. Other than silvers the solid colours were favourites, and the most highly prized was the blue. Gradually the blue came to be regarded as the epitome of the breed.

After the Second World War there were very few stud males left. As a result some matings were made to cats of less cobby type and the typical sturdy look of the British Shorthair was nearly lost for all time. In the 1950s breeders attempted to reverse the damage by mating out to Persians. The massive type of the Persian virtually saved the British Shorthair breed and it became the norm to mate out to Persian every fifth generation. Later most breeders began to select for type within the breed and to evolve lines of cats with British Shorthairs only.

Conformation
Compact and powerful body with rather short legs and a thick tail with a rounded tip. The head is round with smallish ears and large wide-open eyes. In the British GCCF the British Shorthair is required to have a straight nose but in other associations the nose is described as having a slight dip at eye level. In practice most British Shorthairs registered with the GCCF have this slight dip in profile despite the breed standard requirements.

Coat
Fairly short and crisp to the touch.

Colours
White; black; blue; chocolate; lilac; red; cream; black tortie; blue tortie; chocolate tortie; lilac tortie; black tabby; blue tabby; chocolate tabby; lilac tabby; red tabby; cream tabby; black golden tabby; blue golden tabby; chocolate golden tabby; lilac golden tabby; black silver tabby; blue silver tabby; chocolate silver tabby; lilac silver tabby; black/white; blue/white; chocolate/white; lilac/white; black tortie/white; blue tortie/white; chocolate tortie/white; lilac tortie/white; black smoke; blue smoke; chocolate smoke; lilac smoke; cameo smoke; cream cameo smoke; black shaded silver; blue shaded silver; chocolate shaded silver; lilac shaded silver; shaded cameo; shaded cream cameo; black tipped silver; blue tipped silver; chocolate tipped silver; lilac tipped silver; seal point; blue point; chocolate point; lilac point; red point; cream point; seal tortie point; blue tortie point; chocolate tortie point; lilac tortie point; seal tabby point; lilac tabby point; red tabby point; cream tabby point. Some associations recognize patched tabbies (torbies) in addition to the above. Others recognize only some of the colours listed.

Patterns
Solids; classic (blotched) tabby; mackerel tabby; spotted tabby; ticked tabby; tortie; bi-colour; harlequin; van; tortie and white; shaded; chinchilla (tipped); colourpoint; smoke.

Eyes
Usually orange or copper, except in whites where it may be blue, orange or one eye blue and the other orange.

Variation
Very little but blacks sometimes look rather brownish following prolonged exposure to sunlight.

Personality
Prosaic and stolid.

Voice
Varies between cats but usually quiet.

Kittens
Most colours are born wearing their adult coats, except that pointed cats are born white.

Show Status
Recognized worldwide and shown in Britain, USA, Japan, all countries of the FIFe and the independent cat clubs of Europe.

Breeding
No other breed allowed in pedigrees for full Stud Book registration by FIFe or in the USA. Persians still allowed in pedigrees in Britain.

Red classic tabby British Shorthair

Chartreux

Name
Named either for the Carthusian monks or because its colour resembled the *pile de Chartreux*, a wool imported into France from Spain. Also known as Certosino in Italy and Karthuizer in the Netherlands.

Origins
The Chartreux is an ancient French variety of domestic cat and it is widely believed that the Carthusian monks were famous, not only for their liqueur, but also for their highly-prized blue cats. The first written mention of the Chartreux is found in a French poem of 1558 when Joachim du Bellay described his cat Bellaud as similar to the grey cats that were common in France. The 1723 edition of the *Universal Dictionary of Commerce, of Natural History and of the Arts and Trades* stated that 'Chartreux' was in common use as a name for cats with grey-blue coats. According to Pocock in his paper given to the Zoological Society of London in 1907 the title *Felis catus caeruleus* was given to 'the blue-grey cats from Europe and Siberia' in 1777, thus suggesting that the blue cats from which the present-day Russian Blue has evolved and the Chartreux may have a common origin.

The Chartreux as a show cat was developed comparatively recently. In 1928 a breeding project was commenced by Mlle Leger and her sister who owned the de Guerveur cattery. When they moved to Belle-Ile-sur-Mer they took particular notice of the grey cats known locally as 'hospital cats' because they roamed free in the grounds of the hospital. They decided to acquire some and to develop them as a breed. At the end of the war period the remnants of the Chartreux breed were in a sorry state, with very few cats of documented ancestry left. Finally breeders realized that the only way to re-establish the breed would be virtually to start again by using native blue non-pedigree cats and evolving a programme of selective breeding to the pre-war breed standard.

In 1970 Helen Gamon of California formed a US breeders' group to import from France. Ten cats made their way across the Atlantic, three of them being from the original de Guerveur cattery. The new enthusiasts set about a breeding programme designed to produce pure-bred Chartreux and within a few years had achieved championship status in most US associations. Now the Chartreux is better established in the USA than in any other country except France.

Folklore
Legends concerning the origin of the Chartreux abound, the most popular being that a Carthusian monk carried one home after a visit to South Africa. Also often repeated is the story that the Carthusians were given their cats by knights returning from the Crusades.

Conformation
Described by an American breeder as resembling a potato on toothpicks, the Chartreux has a large, well-muscled body on rather finely-boned legs. The head is broad and large but not round as in the British Shorthair. Ears are of medium size and set upright. The breed standard of the American CFA describes its body type as 'primitive', neither cobby nor classic.

Coat
Dense medium-short coat which may part at the neck and on the flanks like the wool of a sheepskin. The longer protective topcoat of guard hairs sits on a shorter, resilient and slightly woolly undercoat. Females may have a silkier thinner coat.

Colours
The blue-grey coat varies in tone between cats and any shade is allowed within the range of ash grey to slate grey. Ideally the coat should be tipped with silver to give an iridescent sheen and any irregularity in tone is regarded as a fault. No other colour is accepted in the breed and judges are required to withhold championships from cats showing white lockets of fur beneath the chin or at the groin.

Patterns
Solid colour only. Any ghost tabby pattern is regarded as a fault.

Eyes
A clear brilliant orange.

Variation
Coat texture and degree of woolliness may vary according to sex, age and environment. Mature males tend to have the heaviest coats. Coat colour may become rusty just before the moult. Eye colour fades with age and, in females, after kittening.

Personality
According to Fernand Mery, in *The Life, History and Magic of the Cat*: 'The Chartreux accommodates itself to everything. It is a simple and good-natured peasant, but a sure friend.'

Voice
Gentle voice but rarely used. Said to chirp rather than miaow and to purr with a deep buzz.

Kittens
Born blue. Their eye colour develops gradually over the first few months of life from baby blue, through brownish-grey to orange or copper.

Show Status
Recognized as championship breed by all the associations of the USA; by all the countries of the FIFe; and by the CA of Britain. Not recognized by the GCCF. Shown in all European countries; USA, Canada and Japan.

Breeding
Pedigrees with only Chartreux for at least three generations are preferred.

Domestic Cat

Name
Also known as House cat, Street cat, Garage cat or Moggie.

Origins
Researchers now agree that the present-day domestic cat shares its ancestry with the pedigree breeds and that this ancestry is the warm-climate African wildcat (*Felis silvestris lybica*) and the cold-climate European wildcat (*Felis silvestris silvestris*).

It is likely that the African wildcat was the first to become domesticated and that it then interbred with the European wildcat. This theory is supported by the fact that matings between African and European wildcats produce kittens closely resembling the domestic striped tabby, and by the fact that in the wildcats of the Middle East there is an intermingling between the warm-climate and the cold-climate types so that it is difficult to decide by sight alone if a cat is a feral domestic or a wild one.

About the time when humans first began to farm and settle into villages cats scavenged around grain stores for small rodents and then began to venture closer to steal scraps from the humans' meals. It was probably about this time that the cat cultivated a taste for cooked meat and fish as well as the raw variety it could obtain by hunting. Later still, as dairy farming became established in Egypt and Iran, the cat developed a taste for milk. Interestingly there are large areas of central Africa and eastern Asia where there is no tradition of milking and both humans and cats from these areas are unable to digest and absorb milk sugars.

The Egyptians' interest in animals led them to keep and breed cats in their temples and in their homes. The numbers became so high that they inevitably spread to Crete, mainland Greece, Libya, India and China. When the Romans invaded and subdued the Egyptians and Christianity replaced the old Egyptian gods the cat was freed from religious duties and became a household pet/rodent killer. In that capacity it was kept by the Romans who were responsible for its spread to Europe.

How did the mild-mannered domestic cat evolve from the ferocious wildcat? When any wild mammal is first domesticated and bred in captivity its skeleton becomes gradually smaller with every generation. The cat developed a reduced brain size, more body fat, a softer coat and a more submissive personality. When mutations first occurred to produce the non-agouti coat and different colours and patterns these affected the hormonal system too, producing cats which were less aggressive and more tolerant of living in close proximity with others. Mutation to other colours and patterns also occurred and the fact that some of these were preferred by man affected the breeding of domestic cats so that they could be classified into three groups – those of the cat fancy whose breeding is completely controlled by humans; those of the general urban populations where mating is indiscriminate but where human selection plays a part in the decision as to which kittens reach maturity and which are 'put down', and farm cats or cats which have returned to live in the wild (feral) where there is no human control over selection of mate or of kittens reared.

In recent years the worldwide 'moggie spotting' activities of geneticists have revealed that the second group of cats have probably changed very little in the last 2,000 years, although there has been a cosmopolitan mixing of genetic stock due to the increased opportunities for humans to travel. The earliest colour mutations are tabby, black, blue, orange (red or ginger) white markings and white. Black is believed to have originated in the eastern Mediterranean in the Classical period, while the blotched (classic) tabby, with its wide stripes and whorls, had a relatively recent origin, possibly in Britain in Elizabethan times. Orange is believed to have mutated in Asia Minor and longhair first occurred in Russia.

Conformation
Moderate in all respects with a fairly long body, well muscled in un-neutered cats but often covered with a soft fatty layer in neuters. Medium long legs and a tail usually reaching to the shoulder. In European domestic cats there is a strong resemblance to the cold climate form of wildcat. In domestic cats of other parts of the world body build may be lighter, the cat may be smaller generally and the tail may be kinked.

Coat
Of medium soft texture. Either medium short or medium long.

Colours and Patterns
All colours, patterns and colour/pattern combinations.

Eyes
All colours.

Personality
Non-aggressive, sometimes timid but usually affectionate.

Voice
Usually quiet in European-type domestic cats. Louder in Asian-type domestic cats.

Kittens
In European-type cats kittens are relatively slow to develop and open their eyes between seven to ten days, moving around their bed from about four weeks. In Asian-type cats kittens open their eyes at about five to seven days, begin to climb around at about three weeks and are usually investigating their surroundings by the age of four weeks.

Show status
The Domestic cat was the first show cat and still holds pride of place in many show halls. Most cat show organizations make special provision for pet cats and several of them offer special titles. The two most important are the Master and Grand Master titles of TICA in the USA and the Laureate, Laureate Prima and Laureate Suprema titles of the CA in Britain. The CA also holds specialist pet cat shows.

European Shorthair

Name
The name indicates that the breed has evolved from domestic cats of Europe.

Origins
The selective breeding of cats began during the second half of the nineteenth century as a direct result of the publication of Darwin's 1868 work, *The variation of animals and plants under domestication*, and of the increased leisure time of many of the population. Before that, shorthair cats had been kept as pets but their breeding had been left to chance. From their earliest days as show cats the shorthairs of Britain and Europe were defined as those with stocky build, large heads and dense thick coats, and there was little difference between the English or British cats and the Europeans. For many years the terms British Shorthair and European Shorthair were interchangeable and judges assessed both breeds to the same standards. The evolution of the European dates from the time when show organizers first classified domestic cats and European/British cats separately, and then re-named the domestic cats as European in 1982, allocating differing standards for British and European. Selective breeding has now established it as a definite breed in its own right but although there are clear differences between good examples of both breeds the fact that many cats fall below the ideal means that there remains some confusion over classification on appearance alone.

Conformation
A rather stocky cat with a medium-length body set on strong, rather thick legs and strong, round paws. The tail is of medium length so that ideally it reaches to just between the base of the rib-cage and the shoulder. The head, like that of the generally cobbier British Shorthair, is rounded but the muzzle is slightly longer so that overall the head is a little longer than wide. Seen from the side the nose has a slight indentation at the level of the eyes.

Coat
Short and very thick with a firm feel when touched.

Colours
White with blue eyes; white with orange eyes; white with one eye blue and one eye orange; black; blue; chocolate; lilac; red; cream; black tortie; blue tortie; black tabby; blue tabby; red tabby; cream tabby; black silver tabby; blue silver tabby; black tortie; blue tortie; chocolate tortie; lilac tortie; black and white; blue and white; black tortie and white; blue tortie and white; red and white; cream and white.

Patterns
Solids; blotched, mackerel and spotted tabby; tortoiseshell; bi-colour.

Eyes
Blue or orange or odd eyes colour in whites; green, gold or orange copper in all other varieties.

Variation
Tabby patterns lose distinction at the time of the moult. Black coat often has a rusty tinge following exposure to strong sunlight. Blue coat often has a brownish tinge at the time of the moult.

Personality
A moderate, sensible cat.

Voice
Varies but is usually quiet.

Kittens
Born with their mature colour and pattern, although tabbies will appear much darker at birth and patterns will be blurred.

Show Status
Recognized as a championship breed in all countries of FIFe; in the independent clubs of Europe; in Britain by the CA. Shown throughout Europe.

Breeding
Only European Shorthairs are allowed in pedigrees for the full Stud Book although Europeans of unknown pedigree may be entered into pedigree classes if adjudged excellent by two judges in a novice or determination class.

Black Tortoiseshell European Shorthair

Exotic Shorthair

Name
The name was chosen in the USA to define it separately from the American Shorthairs because of its part-Persian ancestry.

Origins
Just as Persians were often used as mates for British and European Shorthairs in an effort to rebuild those breeds after the Second World War, so were they mated with American Shorthairs in the USA. The intention was to bring a more Persian look to the rather 'plain Jane' American Shorthairs of that time. Matings between American Shorthairs and Persians became so common that it was frequently stated that the only true American Shorthairs were to be found in the non-pedigree classes. Eventually it became clear that a new breed had been inadvertently created. American Shorthair breeders were adamant – they did not want to change their breed standard to fit the new-look cats, even though the majority of American Shorthairs no longer fitted that standard. The result was stalemate, until in 1966 Jane Martinke suggested that a new class should be created for the American Shorthair/Persian hybrids. The name given to cats in the new class was 'Exotic'. In 1967 the Exotic was shown for the first time and it immediately found favour with breeders and the general public. In 1969 Bob and Nancy Lane of the Leprechaun cattery started the first Exotic breed club and, together with other pioneer fanciers, they set about establishing the breed.

Conformation
Identical to the Persians in conformation with a large, broad, round head and medium-length cobby body set on short, strong legs. The tail is short and thick.

Coat
Soft, plushy and dense with length intermediate to that of the American Shorthair and the Persians so that the breed is often referred to as 'the Persian in its petticoat'.

Colours and Patterns
All the colours and patterns of the Persian are found in the Exotic Shorthair.

Eyes
Eye colour varies with coat colour but except in whites is generally copper. Whites may have copper eyes, blue eyes or one eye copper and the other blue.

Variation
Although Exotics do not have the same dramatic moult as their Persian cousins they do lose a great deal more coat in the early summer than American Shorthairs. Conversely the amount of undercoat increases in cold weather.

Personality
Bright and alert yet quiet and gentle. A breed that gets along well with people and other cats.

Voice
Quiet, similar to the Persian.

Kittens
Born with coats very similar to those of the Persian but the coat characteristics become more obvious over the first few weeks. Exotic kittens are very lazy, often showing no desire to move from the nest until they are over three weeks old.

Show Status
A championship breed in most associations other than in the British GCCF. Shown in all countries of the FIFe, USA, Canada, Japan, Britain and the Baltic States.

Breeding
Only Persians, Exotics and American Shorthair allowed in pedigrees in the USA, Canada or Japan. Only Persians, Exotics and European or British Shorthair allowed in pedigrees elsewhere.

Golden shaded Exotic Shorthair

Manx

Name
Named after the Isle of Man where the breed is believed to have originated.

Origins
The Manx is widely believed to have arisen by mutation among domestic cats on the Isle of Man because tailless cats were first described here. During the early days of the cat fancy in Britain the Manx was very popular. The first recorded champion was Bonhaki, a silver tabby male. The Manx Cat Club was formed in 1901 and when the Governing Council of the Cat Fancy was inaugurated in Britain its first secretary, Gambier Bolton, was a Manx breeder.

When Manx first went to the USA is not quite clear as many were imported from Britain as pets before pedigree registries were opened. Notable among Manx breeders in the USA were Ellen and Ruth Carlson of Illinois who started showing in 1933, and Manx became one of the first breeds recognized by the CFA prior to 1951. In the last years of the 1980s two of CFA's top ten cats were Manx. Despite the many difficulties of breeding Manx the breed has become established firmly as a top show cat of the 1990s.

The taillessness of the Manx is caused by a gene which affects the whole spinal column and the central nervous system. The fact that the gene has variable expression means that Manx are conventionally classified into four types: Rumpy Manx, with rounded hindquarters and complete absence of tail; Rumpy-riser Manx, with immoveable rudimentary tail vertebrae; Stumpie Manx, with a short tail, often deformed but usually moveable; and Longie Manx, with a short but otherwise fairly normal tail.

Folklore
Legends concerning the Manx abound. Some say that the breed descended from two cats who were the last to board Noah's Ark with the result that Noah, impatient to beat the weather, slammed the door on their tails. Others believe that Manx swam ashore from sinking vessels of the Spanish Armada. Another story is that Irish invaders cut the tails off the local Manx cats to use them to decorate their helmets and mother cats bit off their kittens' tails to prevent them. Finally, another story, once widely believed, is that a cat was mated by a rabbit, the resulting kittits or rabbins having the rabbit's tail and its hopping gait.

Conformation
A cat of medium bone structure, muscular and strong, giving an effect of roundness as a result of the rather short back which arches from the shoulders to rounded haunches. The Manx head is large, with prominent cheeks, a moderately long nose and a strong muzzle. The ears are fairly large, set quite high on the head but with a slight outward angle.

Coat
Thick, plus undercoat, rather short, underlying a coarser topcoat which is longer and more open. Sometimes described as a 'double coat'.

Colours
All colours.

Patterns
All patterns are acceptable in most associations although some will not admit Siamese-pattern Manx.

Eyes
Usually in keeping with the coat colour.

Variation
Undercoat moults out in the summer season, making the coat flatter overall.

Personality
Sweet and undemanding, making faithful slaves of their owners.

Voice
Melodious.

Kittens
Born with the tail type or lack of tail they will keep through life.

Show Status
One of the oldest breeds, recognized for championships and shown worldwide since the dawn of the cat fancy.

Breeding
Only Manx are allowed in pedigrees for the full Stud Book registration in the USA and the countries of FIFe although all degrees of Manx are allowed. In Britain outcrosses to selected other breeds are allowed.

Silver classic tabby Manx

Scottish Fold

Name
Named after its country of origin. Once known as Lop-eared cats.

Origins
In 1951 a white female kitten with folded ears was born in a litter of farm cats near Coupar Angus in the Tayside region of Scotland. She adopted Mr and Mrs McCrae, who lived in a nearby cottage and who treasured her for her odd pixie-like expression and unusual ears. They named her Susie. When fully grown she was noticed by William Ross, the shepherd from a neighbouring farm. He showed her to his wife Mary and they asked the McCraes to let them have a folded-ear kitten should Susie ever produce one. After a wait of two years they were able to acquire Snooks, also white, who was to become the founder of the breed. The Rosses registered Denisla as their cattery name and mated Snooks to a red tabby domestic cat. The resultant litter included a white male with folded ears. They named him Snowball and mated him to a white shorthair named Lady May to produce, among others, Denisla Snowdrift. Next the Rosses mated Snooks to a full pedigree British Shorthair Blue. She produced a litter of five kittens which, together with those from matings made by Patricia Turner to her champion British White Shorthair Scarletina Diamond, produced progeny to found breeding lines for all the early British breeders.

The fact that some Fold kittens had short, thick tails with rounded tips and rather thick limbs was noticed at the very beginning. Breeders were encouraged to breed even more selectively, outcrossing to widen the gene pool, introduce new colours and improve body type. This practice is continued today. In Britain's CA registration of Folds is only available to cats with one non-Fold parent. This breeding policy, combined with the faulting of over-thick limbs and thickened, short inflexible tails in the show ring has allowed the Fold to evolve as a breed well-known in every country of the world except Scotland! In Scotland there are now only one or two breeders left. It was not until the CA of Britain was formed in 1983 and held a championship show in Scotland in 1984 that the Scottish Fold achieved recognition in its native land.

Conformation
A compact, solidly-padded breed with a short, thick body set on legs which, although strong and firm, should not be over cobby. The ideal tail is rather long and definitely flexible and tapering – just like the tail of a domestic cat.

The head is set on a rather short, strong, thick neck and the head overall gives the impression of being containable within an imaginery circle. The ears are set normally but the ear flaps are tightly folded so that the tops of the ears point towards the nose.

Coat
A rather short, dense, resilient coat with texture varying slightly between different colour varieties but generally rather soft to the touch.

Colours and Patterns
Most colours other than chocolate, lilac or seal and most patterns other than Siamese pattern. The most popular patterns are those of bi-colour or harlequin.

Eyes
In keeping with coat colour although whites may have deep blue or bright golden eyes or even one blue and one golden.

Variation
Very little except that blues develop a rusty look just before the main moult and blacks may develop brownish areas if exposed to prolonged sunlight.

Personality
Placid and good-natured. A good mixer with other cats, dogs or humans.

Voice
Fairly quiet except when calling for a mate.

Kittens
New-born kittens are virtually identical to kittens of domestic cats but after a few days those with shorter thicker tails can be easily detected. Ears are normal for the first two weeks, after which they begin to fold over towards the front.

Show Status
Recognized for championship competition by the CFA of America and TICA; by the CA of Britain; in Japan, New Zealand, Australia, Germany, Holland, France and most countries of Europe. Shown worldwide.

Cameo classic tabby Scottish Fold

The Persian Group

Peter Warner

The Persian group includes all the varieties developed from cats imported from Turkey, Persia (now Iran), Afghanistan and Russia at the turn of the eighteenth and nineteenth centuries. Some have colour mostly restricted to the points and others have colour and pattern dispersed all over the body.

A number of explanations have been proposed for the origin of the longhair cat. It was once thought to have descended from either Pallas's cat, *Felis manul*, or the sand cat, *Felis margarita*. However, scientific studies have now proved that the gene for long hair must have mutated in domestic cats in Russia, descended from the heavy, long haired cold-climate *Felis silvestris*.

Even before cats were appreciated as pets and for show, the longhair cats from Russia, being unusual in appearance as well as equally expert in the killing of vermin, would have been more highly prized than shorthairs. They spred into Asia Minor on trading ships, and as they reached the

habitat of the warm-climate domestics they inter-mated with them, giving rise to typical Turkish longhair.

The Russian longhairs, travelling by a shorter route to Persia (now Iran), retained more of the original cold-climate form, with a heavier body, dense undercoat and coarser stapled hair to become the cats that we now know as Persians. The Persians were not always cat lovers. A story is told that in 595 BC when the Persians were besieging Pelusia, on the Egyptian border, the Persian King, knowing that the Egyptians revered cats and would not dare to kill them, ordered his soldiers to attach cats to their shields. The Egyptians dared not counter-attack for fear of hurting the cats. This ruse is said to have allowed the Persian army to conquer Pelusia.

Longhair cats were taken from Turkey to France by the naturalist Fabri de Pereise in the sixteenth century. These early longhairs were called

Angora cats, after the Turkish city of Angora, or French cats, after their country of adoption. In the late eighteenth century more longhair cats with coarser, denser coats, and a stockier build were imported into Britain from Persia and Afghanistan. Some records indicate that cats were also imported directly from Russia. Cats imported from Turkey were mostly whites while those imported from Russia, Afghanistan and Persia were mostly black or blue. The Angora cats had less of an undercoat and a shorter, though silkier top coat. Once cat shows were established it became apparent that the cats most likely to win prizes were those combining the merits of both. In whites it was noticed that the cats with the deepest blue eyes were often the ones with the longest noses; so breeders cross-bred with shorter-nosed blacks, blues and fawns (creams). The result was that blue eyes were often replaced by orange eyes, but shorter noses resulted. Some whites had odd eyes, with one eye orange and the other blue.

Gradually the breed evolved to have longer hair, a denser undercoat, a wider, flatter face, shorter nose, smaller, wider-set ears, a shorter body and tail and bigger, rounder eyes. The lighter-bodied type of the Angoras had been lost, although in 1900 new imports direct from Turkey to the USA allowed for eventual re-recognition of the breed. By 1980 in the USA and 1990 in Europe the state of the Persian cat mirrored that of the Siamese: the present-day type bears little or no resemblance to the original imports. But just as there is now a move in the USA to re-recognize the 'traditional Siamese', so the Russians plan to obtain recognition for the progenitor of the Persian in the beautiful 'Siberian', a cat with a moderately heavy body, a dense undercoat and a long, rather coarse stapled top coat. The wheel has turned full circle.

When Harrison Weir organized the first cat shows he classified longhair and shorthair cats but always preferred the shorthairs. Not until Frances Simpson and others championed the Persian did the breed start to come into its own in Britain. Most judges were 'all rounders' who judged not only all breeds of cat but also birds, dogs, flowers and so on. The weekly magazine *Fur and Feather* first appeared in 1890 and Persians began to appear in its For Sale columns. At the same time in the USA Mr C. H. Jones launched the monthly *Cat Journal*, which was probably the first magazine in the world devoted exclusively to cats.

Black Persians were in the majority at that time and they were used in the breeding of a myriad of other colours. There were several noted examples of the cross between blacks with blues, including the famous Champion Dirty Dick. The breed standard for black required coats as black as the proverbial jet, round eyes of deep orange colour, and big massive build. Faults were white lockets or bars.

But blue Persians soon became the most popular. Size was considered very important and the weight of kittens was often included in advertisements. The first blues exhibited were owned by Frances Simpson. As there were no special blue classes her exhibits were entered as 'Any other colour'. In 1889 blues were given their own class under the name 'Blue self – without white'. Within a year entries were high enough to warrant splitting the adult cat classes into males and females.

Several Persians were present at the first American show at the Madison Square Garden, New York, in 1895. They included King Humbert, Topaz and Minnie, all tabbies, and The Banshee, a white. At the British National Cat Show of 1879 Persians with coat colours including white, tortie and white, a 'strangely graduated grey' and silver tabby were described. Silvers were also very popular in the USA where King of the Silvers, Jack Frost, Bitterne Silver Chieftain and an import from Britain named Silver Belle all became champions.

In Canada the pioneer Persian breeders were Mrs Cumberland of Port Hope, Ontario and an Englishman, Mr A. Burland. All colours were bred and many cats were imported from England. Ireland too exported cats to Canada. In 1906 a Canadian writer described 'Prince, a grand old cat imported from Ireland seven years ago and there are few cats extant today, or ever were, that can take his measure. His head is magnificent, and he is short on the leg, has plenty of bone, grand colour, no weak colouring around the lips or chin and, what is more, he sires the right sort.'

California was said to be too warm for longhairs and their coat parasites were thought to be too prevalent to make the rearing or caring for longhairs 'a pleasant occupation'. It was believed that the best cats came from England and that the crossing of native cats with English cats was particularly successful. Many American cats were said to fail in type of quality.

In Britain the blue creams had been known for many years as 'blue and cream mixed' and it was not until 1929 that they were formally recognized as a breed. The first champion was Judy of Cardonald, bred by Miss Darlington-Manley. In the USA the variety was shown under the name blue tortoiseshell or blue tortie; but by 1931 the Americans had adopted the British name of blue cream. The two fancies have different requirements for coat pattern – the British requiring the two colours to be 'gently intermingled', while the Americans stipulate clearly defined patches.

Creams were first known as fawns or, more derisively, as 'spoiled oranges', and were originally much darker in colour than they are today. The first fawn recorded was Cupid Bassanio in 1890 and early winners were Romaldkirk Admiral, Romaldkirk Midshipmite and Matthew of the Durhams. In the 1920s a cat named Champion John Barleycorn, owned by Mrs Clive Behrens, reigned supreme. American fanciers always liked the creams, and when the famous Kew Laddie crossed the Atlantic from Britain he was a big success, siring many kittens and winning multiple show honours. The original breeders preferred unmarked creams, and cats showing tabby markings were faulted at shows. But in 1983 the CA of Britain and the member countries of FIFe agreed to offer championships to the cream tabby Persian too.

The red self, originally known as orange, was popular from the very beginning of the fancy. At first classified with the creams and then with the tabbies, it was eventually given its own show class, firstly as orange longhair, then as red or orange longhair, with a separate class for red or orange tabby longhairs. By 1915 there were classes for red self or shaded and for red tabbies. A well known winner at that time was Mrs Western's

Wynnstay Ruddiman. Just before the Second World War Germany was the home of some of the best reds ever bred. The war years took their toll of cats as well as humans and it was almost twenty years before the variety regained its former quality.

In the USA breeders began to develop an excessively short-faced variety of red, which was recognized under the name Pekeface Persian because of its similarity to the Pekingese dog. Although this variety is officially recognized only in the USA many new strains of Persian (other than the tabbies, shaded silvers and chinchillas) appear to be evolving with a similar head type, notably the Himalayan Persian (see page 46).

Smoke Persians were first described in 1860 but their genetics were not understood and they were believed to result from matings between blacks, blues and whites. The first Persian stud list, drawn up in Britain in 1912, included eighteen smokes. They were allocated a class of their own in 1893 and the first smoke champion was Backwell Jogram, owned by Mrs H. V. James. A beautiful cat, though completely different to the wonderful smokes of today, he appears from photographs to bear a striking resemblance in type to the Siberian of Russia. Although the first smokes were either black or blue, more recently the colour range was extended to include smoke torties in black, blue, chocolate and lilac, and also red smokes and cream smokes.

Tabby Persians were also very popular: it was Miss Southam's famous Birkdale Ruffie who swept the board at the 1896 Crystal Palace show and won the coveted Prince of Wales prize. Frances Simpson was particularly fond of the black-marked tabbies which were then known, as they still are today in the GCCF, as brown tabbies. She owned the famous Champion Persimmon. But even after such an auspicious beginning the variety lost popularity and nearly died out. Due to the interest taken by a number of notable breeders it was partially revived but has never been seen in large numbers in its original colour. Blue tabby Persians with their pale blue marked ivory coats have attracted a great deal of attention in more recent years although they remain relatively rare. They were recognized in the USA in 1962 and by the FIFe in 1977.

Silver tabby Persians were always in demand in the early years of the cat fancy. They have never developed into the excessively short-nosed type currently fashionable in Persian circles. At shows today the silver can be found in four colour variations – black on silver, blue on silver, chocolate on silver and lilac on silver. Even today the best silver tabbies have silver roots

to the hair, and it was from cats of this variety that 'unsound' or 'spoiled' silver tabbies were first bred to become the ancestors of the silver chinchilla Persians of today.

The earliest chinchillas were the results of matings between unsound silver tabbies and smokes. The name was chosen because of the cat's resemblance to the chinchilla variety of rabbit, and to the South American rodent itself. Over the last hundred years chinchillas have changed from

what would now be known as shaded silvers to the present-day silver-white cats with each hair minimally tipped with black. The wonderful combination of silver coat and green or blue green eyes has attracted cat lovers to this variety since its inception. The best silver chinchillas are now those bred in the USA. Silver chinchillas are shown in a wide range of colours, with the red and cream varieties being known in some countries as cameo. The latter varieties first appeared in the USA in 1934 as a result of matings between silver chinchillas and self reds. A planned breeding programme was commenced in 1950 and the USA associations granted championship status in 1960. The varieties were bred in Europe in the mid 1950s and recognized by the FIFe in 1975.

Although the original silver chinchillas were actually shaded silvers and from 1902 it was recognized that both dark and light chinchillas would occur, the darker variety later became one of the 'unrecognized' breeds. With the typical green eyes of the silver they were eventually standardized in FIFe in 1976 and by the CA of Britain in 1983, but remain a non-championship variety in GCCF where an orange-eyed shaded silver under the name pewter was recognized instead. The differences between the chinchillas and the shaded silver coat are produced by the presence or absence of a single gene (known as wide band). In cats with two wide band genes the coat is chinchilla, whereas cats with only one are shaded. The occurrence of golden chinchilla and shaded golden Persians was reported in the early 1990s, but the varieties were only recognized by FIFe and the CA of Britain in 1983. In the GCCF both varieties are classified together under the name golden Persian. The genetic difference between the silver and golden varieties is simple: the latter lacks the gene that inhibits the formation of yellow pigment, thus producing areas of silver.

At early shows black and white Persians were described as 'Magpies'. They were always shown in the 'Any other colour' class in Britain. In the USA however they were given their own classification in the earliest days of the cat fancy and many lovely cats were bred. Under the name 'bi-colour' they were recognized for championships in Britain in 1966 after years of virtually unaided work by Miss Norah Woodifield. The first British champion was one of her Pathfinders cats. The variety was recognized by the FIFe in 1969 and by the USA CFA in 1971. Persians showing the pattern of the Turkish Van were recognized by the FIFe in 1986 under the name of 'Harlequin' and in the USA as 'Van Pattern Persian'.

A particularly interesting variety of Persian is the tortie and white, which bred in the colours of black tortie/white, blue tortie/white, chocolate tortie/white and lilac tortie/white represents the female equivalent to the bi-colour males. In the USA these cats are known as calicos and were once described as chintz. Although they were always standardized in Britain and Europe they were only recognized for USA championships in 1956.

The history of the Himalayan or Colourpoint Persian is detailed on page 46. Since its emergence chocolate and lilac Persians have become well known at shows, first being recognized in the USA under the breed name Kashmir.

Grooming the Persian is an art. Every colour variety requires slightly different treatment. In all cats it is necessary to keep the coat tangle- and knot-free. The soft hair on the belly and between the legs tends to curl and may easily become knotted. It must be teased rather than brushed, and care must be taken to avoid pulling the skin. A cat that is roughly groomed because the owner has not given it regular attention will resent further handling and the problems will increase.

During the spring and autumn moult the cat swallows dead hairs while grooming itself. They collect in the stomach and form hairballs which do not pass into the intestine but instead are ejected by vomiting. Regular grooming by the owner will prevent this happening too frequently.

Blacks often have a rusty or grey coat until they are at least seven or eight months old. Only after the second moult between a year and eighteen months does the coat change colour to become jet black. White hairs may appear sprinkled throughout the kitten coat but they do tend to disappear – either by falling out when the kitten matures or with the help of their owner. Kittens showing good black coats from the very start of life are later not usually so good in colour as those with the imperfections mentioned. A tendency towards rustiness may be seen in cats with a very soft coat, especially if they are exposed to prolonged sunshine. Patches of white or clusters of white hair tend to remain throughout life and are a serious fault.

In whites the presence of dead white hairs may give an impression of yellowness, as may the presence of excess oil. Whites are usually very carefully bathed before shows, and special blue-tinted shampoos are often used. Optical whiteners in the form of grooming powders are also available. Smudges of coloured hair on the top of the head often occur in kittens but disappear at maturity. These are not considered a fault.

Blue Persians often have profuse coats and can be kept in optimum condition by the regular use of cornstarch (cornflour) as a grooming powder in order to absorb excess grease. In the USA a proprietary de-greasing shampoo is available to exhibitors whose cats' tails are excessively greasy and show the beginnings of acne or 'stud tail'. If stud tail occurs it leaves an unsightly bare area and can only be resolved by constant attention and the use of specialist treatments.

Red Persians are usually prepared for shows by a bran bath (see page 18) and a final gloss is given to the coat with a silk cloth or chamois leather. Powder is not widely used for this variety, nor is it used for smokes, as it dulls the brightness of the coat. Smoke kittens never have the full smoke effect of the adult and judges take this into account. No amount of grooming will produce a silver frill in a kitten under six months of age.

Tabby Persians are not powdered before shows and are groomed so that the coat falls, thus allowing the full tabby pattern effect to be clearly seen. The frill is groomed out from the body to accentuate the head and in the direction of the pattern. Kittens always have darker coloured coats: it is said that the darkest kittens will make the best adults, while kittens with well-marked coats will turn pale and show a blurred pattern after about six months.

The show preparation of the tortie or blue cream in associations requiring the colouring to be mingled is quite an art, involving judicious plucking and very careful grooming. Powder is usually used on the blue cream as this makes the coat appear softer and reduces the colour contrast.

In general, breeders of the Persian varieties give specialist advice on grooming to others of their circle and to buyers of kittens. Novices in Persian ownership are well advised to join a Persian club or to contact an already successful exhibitor for advice.

Himalayan Persian

Name
Known simply as Himalayan in the USA where it was first bred. Named by American breeders to follow the convention of the name Himalayan for Siamese-pointed mice and rabbits. Known as Colourpoint Longhair in the GCCF of Britain and as Colourpoint Persian in the CA of Britain and the member countries of the FIFe. Known colloquially in the USA as Himmies.

Origins
The first breeding programme to combine Siamese blue eyes and coat pattern with longhair was carried out by the Swedish geneticist T. Tjebbes, and in his 1924 report he gave breeding data on matings between white longhair and Siamese. However it was never his intention to develop a new longhair variety for the cat fancy.

In 1930 Dr Clyde Keeler of the Harvard Medical School and Miss Virginia Cobb, a well known breeder who owned the Newton's cattery, commenced a breeding project designed to improve knowledge of cat coat colour genetics and in 1931 a litter of three black shorthairs was born from a mating between a Siamese and a black Persian.

Like the earlier work of Tjebbes the Keeler & Cobb breeding project was designed to provide data for genetic studies and was not continued to provide a new cat fancy breed despite the fact that well known show cats had been used. However the foundations for the Himalayan breed had been laid and the breeding data that Keeler and Cobb produced, together with the correspondence she maintained with breeders throughout the world, led others to consider working to the same formula.

Several breeders became interested in a long-haired variety with Siamese pattern and among them was Margaret Goforth of the Goforth's cattery in San Diego, California. Beginning in 1950 she devoted ten years to developing the breed under the name Himalayan. She used white, blue and black in her breeding programme and among her stud line up was her blue Persian Delphi Blue Splendour of Goforth. The first Himalayan champion in the USA was Goforth's LaChiquita owned by Price Cross.

Having read about the breeding programme of Clyde Keeler and Virginia Cobb Mrs Barton-Wright of England formed the Experimental Breeders Club there in 1935 and commenced a programme of matings based on the pattern set in the USA a few years before. Meanwhile Brian Stirling-Webb of England had considered the possibility of repeating the Keeler/Cobb programme and developing a new Persian variety with Siamese points. By coincidence in 1947 he was shown a female cat with long hair and Siamese points. He acquired the cat and by mating it with a black male purchased from Dorothy Collins, he was able to breed what were known as 'primitive colourpoints' – moderate type longhairs with Siamese coat pattern and blue eyes. Gradually he improved the breed type to that required for Persians.

When Ben and Ann Borret of the Chestermere cattery and cattle ranch in Alberta, Canada, visited Brian Stirling-Webb's cattery in England they became deeply interested in the new breed and resolved to perfect it by planned breeding for Persian type. They began work on a pedigree line that was to become famous throughout the world.

In Germany Frau Henrietta Schafer of the Vogelsberg cattery and Frau Romback of the Robachsburg cattery began to work on the breed.

In France in 1959 Mme Gamichon imported Amaska Blue Masque from Susan Luxford-Watts of England. Other English stock followed and the breed soon became well established.

Conformation
As in all Persians.

Coat
As in all Persians.

Colours
As in the Siamese.

Patterns
As in the Siamese.

Eyes
Blue.

Variation
The Himalayan of the USA and the Colourpoint Persian of Europe are both Persian in conformation but there are substantial differences in the interpretation of the breed standards by judges in the two continents. The top winning Himmies in USA would be considered too extreme in Britain and Europe.

Personality
Sweet natured and happy-go-lucky.

Voice
Quiet and melodious.

Kittens
Born white and plump with eyes closed and short, though fluffy hair. The hair length and the colouring develops gradually and the eyes open to show the permanent blue colour from about ten days.

Show Status
Recognized as a championship breed in Britain in 1955 under the name Colourpoint Longhair, and under the name Himalayan in the USA by the ACFA in 1957. Now a championship breed worldwide.

Breeding
Only Himalayans and other Persians are allowed in pedigrees.

Seal point Himalayan (Colourpoint Persian)

Smoke Persian

Name
Named after Persia (now Iran) which is considered to be the country of origin. The GCCF in Britain classifies it as Smoke Longhair for show purposes. The Persians were once known in England as Asiatic cats.

Origins
Although longhaired cats were known in Europe from the fourteenth century onwards they were Turkish in origin and of Angora type. The first records of longhairs of the heavier-bodied and fuller-coated Persian type are in the eighteenth century when the explorer Pietro della Valle is said to have taken cats to Italy. In the nineteenth century the Persian was introduced to Britain where it was cross-bred with Angoras, thus widening the colour spectrum and sightly changing the coat texture yet retaining the thick woolly undercoat. In 1868 Charles Ross described the Persian as 'a variety with hair very long and very silky, perhaps more than the Cat of Angora; it is however differently coloured.'

When Harrison Weir drew up his 'points of excellence' for judging cats in 1889 he defined differences between the Angora and the Persian. In R. I. Pocock's account of English domestic cats given to the Royal Zoological Society in 1907 he stated that the Persian had a marked shortening and widening of the face. This indicates that the Angora influence had been lost.

The first varieties of Persian to be separately classified were the solid colour varieties referred to in Britain as 'selfs'. The colours recognized were black, white, blue, orange, cream or fawn, and sable. As years went by the orange came to be known as red and the sable disappeared into obscurity, re-emerging only recently as the Golden Persian. Other varieties, including tabbies and smokes, were classified as 'Any Other Variety'.

The first smokes are recorded as being bred from matings between blacks, whites and blues. In 1872 Harrison Weir wrote 'a beauty was shown at Brighton, which was white with black tips to the hair, the white being scarcely visible unless the hair was parted . . .' The following year the smokes were allocated their own classes at British shows and numbers rapidly increased. A famous early champion was Mrs H. V. James's Champion Backwell Jogram who sired a number of outstanding kittens. When the National Cat Club Stud Book for the years 1900–1905 was published the number of smokes listed was sixteen males and fourteen females.

Despite its magnificence the smoke remained a cat for the connoisseur and there were very few specialist breeders. A cat described as 'outstanding' in the 1930s was Mrs Alexander's Champion Suffolk Dumpling who later sired the first smoke bred by Miss Collins of the famous Kala cattery. The Kala kitten became Best Smoke in Show at the National Cat Club Show in 1938, and went on to become Champion Kala Moonflower. Breeding lapsed during the Second World War but in the immediate post war years many famous lines, were evolved, including the Treetops, the Beauvales, the Hardendales, the Wildfells, the Fishermores, the Biancas and the Sonatas.

Although most British breeders preferred the darker smokes in the early years of the variety those in America preferred cats with lighter colour.

Two 'exports' who became well known winners in their new country were Watership Caesar owned by Mrs Thurston and Cossey, owned by Lady Marcus Beresford. Other pioneer breeders in the USA were Mr and Mrs R. Green of the Ja Bob cattery and Mrs T. O'Hara.

Conformation
A large cat with wide shoulders and a cobby body set on short, thick, strong legs. Paws are very large and round and the tail is short and well covered so that it appears bushy. The head is wide across the skull with a round forehead and full cheeks and is crowned by tiny ears.

Coat
Coat is fine textured and glossy with a dense soft undercoat which allows the longer top coat to stand out from the body.

Colours
Black; blue; chocolate; lilac; red; cream; black tortie; blue tortie; chocolate tortie; lilac tortie. *Note.* Associations differ in the colours and patterns accepted. The GCCF of Britain does not recognize chocolate, lilac, chocolate tortie or lilac tortie for championships.

Patterns
Silver undercoat, shading to the relevant basic colour with feet and an unmarked mask of the basic colour.

Eyes
Orange or copper.

Personality
A sweet natured cat but can be stubborn.

Voice
High pitched but soft toned and quiet.

Kittens
Born without any discernible silver undercoat but the best ones show 'clown markings' of silver on the face. As the kitten and the coat grows so does the silvery undercoat become apparent although the coat is not at its best until after the second moult.

Show Status
A championship breed in black and blue since the dawn of the cat fancy. Also recognized in red, cream, black tortie and blue tortie world wide and in additional colours by the countries of the FIFe.

Breeding
Only Persians are allowed in pedigrees although any colour of Persian is generally acceptable. One parent must be Smoke Persian.

Black smoke Persian

Pekeface Persian

Name
Named to denote similarity in head type to that of the Pekingese dog.

Origins
Kittens with their nose bridge flat and appearing to be depressed between the eyes and with high foreheads bulging over the nose to form an extreme stop first occurred in the USA in litters from red and red tabby Persians in the 1930s. In addition to the extreme short nose the kittens developed a fold of skin running from the bridge of the nose to the outer edges of the cheeks and, as a result of the shorter nose the structure of the nasal bones and upper jaw was changed so that eyes were frequently runny due to blockages of the tear ducts. Many of the kittens had undershot jaws which could not completely meet the shortened upper jaw. Most breeders considered such kittens to be deformed but a few others found them attractive enough to try to preserve these changed characteristics and to attempt to develop them into a show variety of Persian. Pioneer breeders were Mabel Davidson (Lafeyette cattery), Mrs Earl Posey (Polychrome cattery), Mrs W. R. More (Kootenai cattery), Ella Conroy (Elco cattery) and Mrs Eugene Fouque (McInley Park) and by the 1970s the Tab-B-Town, Smithway, Aristocat and Hedgeway catteries were breeding and promoting the variety.

   The Pekeface never found favour outside America but was granted championship status as a variety of Persian. The difficulties of breeding and the fact that some kittens do not survive because of inability to suckle or as a result of upper respiratory problems has always kept the Pekeface a minority breed and it is now seen only infrequently at shows. However the movement towards the extreme flat faced and short bodied Persians in other colours which started in the USA and has gained momentum in Europe has resulted in some cats of many other colours being very similar in type to the early Pekeface.

Conformation
A massive cobby type body set on sturdy legs and with a short, full coated tail. The head is reminiscent of the head of a Pekingese dog and is described in the breed standard as having a nose that is short, depressed and indented between the eyes; a wrinkled muzzle, and with a horizontal 'break' across the head above the eyes.

Coat
Long and thick, standing out from the body and with an immense ruff and a full brush.

Colours
Red only.

Patterns
Solid and tabby.

Eyes
Brilliant copper.

Personality
Usually sweet natured.

Voice
Soft and quiet.

Kittens
Some kittens are born with obvious peke-faced heads and in extreme cases may be unable to suckle normally. Other kittens appear normal until about the age of six months.

Show Status
A Championship variety of the Persian in the USA only.

Breeding
Only Persians are allowed in pedigrees.

Red classic tabby Pekeface Persian

The Foreign Shorthair Group

The Foreign Shorthair group includes all those short-haired, slender-boned cats that have evolved from the warm climate wildcats. Four of the breeds are Burmese-derived, two more are ancient breeds of the Orient, and most of the remainder are breeds contrived by man or evolving from small wildcats. Not otherwise classifiable is the hairless cat known as the Sphynx.

The oldest breeds in the group in cat fancy terms are the Russian and the Abyssinian and there was considerable controversy about the origins of both. Although everyone agrees that the Abyssinian is very similar in appearance to the domesticated cats of ancient Egypt, the story of its origin in Abyssinia (now Ethiopia) is unlikely to be true. Studies by the geneticist Neil Todd indicate that the gene concerned mutated somewhere in the area of the Bay of Bengal or Ceylon, with the trade routes between there, Burma and Western Malaysia accounting for its presence in such large numbers in those areas.

Although a standard was drawn up for the instruction of judges and breeders at the time of the first Crystal Palace show and championships were offered from 1882 in Britain, expert opinion was that it was 'difficult to isolate the true Abyssinian'. Early breeders of Abyssinians reported that there was a tendency for cats to be too dark and too heavily striped on the limbs. This is now explained by the fact that the gene involved is incompletely dominant. The dark, striped Abyssinians of the 1880s were likely to have been the cats with only one gene for the tabby pattern and would have had the coat pattern now standardized as Ticked Tabby in the Oriental group. Only when Abyssinians were repeatedly mated like to like did the lighter coat, free from striping on the tail and limbs, evolve.

Writing in the 1903 *Book of the Cat*, H. C. Brooke, a famous exhibitor, breeder and judge of the time, commented: 'The colour of an Abyssinian should be a sort of reddish fawn, each individual hair being ticked like that of a wild rabbit – hence the popular name of "bunny" cat.' Brooke was an outspoken critic of his fellow judges, complaining that

> The Cat Club has persistently neglected them [the Abyssinians], having on almost every occasion handed them over to some all-round judge who knows little and cares less about them, with the natural result that exhibitors are disgusted. Take, for instance, the last show, when a very dark, almost sooty Abyssinian was placed above a very fair specimen merely because the latter had about a dozen white hairs on its throat! The value of the winner may be gauged from the fact that the owner, a lady well known in the cat world, expressed her intention of having him neutered and keeping him merely as a pet.

In recent years several new varieties of Abyssinian coat pattern have been introduced from southern Asia: the Singapura (see page 76), the provisionally named Wild Abyssinian and the Celonese. The Wild Abyssinian is a feral cat of Singapore and is bred only in ruddy colouring. Its coat has residual barring on the legs and ringing on the tail and it is appreciably larger than contemporary exhibition Abyssinians. A small group of USA breeders led by Tord Svenson of Massachusetts is breeding the Wild Abyssinian and a breeding policy requiring that every cat registered must have an import within five generations has been designed to avoid inbreeding.

The Celonese, which as a cat fancy breed originated in the Cat Club of Ceylon, is now championed by Italian fanciers and bred in a variety of colours with the ticked tabby pattern and barred legs very similar to that of the original Abyssinians exhibited in the late nineteenth century.

The Celonese and the Wild Abyssinian probably represent the parental types of our present-day Abyssinians, thus mirroring the situation of the Traditional Siamese in the Oriental group and the Siberian in the Semi-Longhair group. The contemporary exhibition Abyssinian has evolved with a virtually unmarked agouti coat and a shorter head, particularly in the USA.

The story of the origin of the Singapura in the USA cat fancy is challenged by the Singapore Cat Club, but cats certified to be pure Singapura by certificates of recognition issued by the club are now also

selectively bred in the USA. The Singapura, as it is known in Europe and some catteries in the USA, represents a derivative of the Abyssinian and Burmese, having originated from crosses between these two breeds. The cats bred from these programmes fit the Singapura standard well although they are normal size cats.

The Egyptian Mau (see page 64) also claims similarity to the cat of the Egyptians and has become very popular in the USA where more than 1,000 cats have been registered by the CFA. It is interesting that one fault requiring disqualification is that of blue eyes. Blue eyes do occur rarely in tipped silvers and it can only be conjectured that the variety showing blue eyes occasionally would be silver.

When the Russian was first exhibited it was said to be a breed protected and kept by the Tsars; but there is no hard evidence to support this story, nor that of the Cossacks riding out at night by torchlight with the cats clinging to their shoulders. The breed made its first appearance in Britain at the Crystal Palace show in 1875 and was described as 'a very handsome cat coming from Arkhangel. They should be particularly furry and give traces of their semi-polar origin, but they do not; they resemble mostly the common grey wild rabbit. They leave the long loose furry habit to the Persian and Angora cats.' At that time most Russians were blue. Kola, a cat from the Kola Peninsula, just north of Arkhangel, was actually blue and white. Her owner, Mrs Carew-Cox, recalled: 'Kola changed hands on the high seas several times and was traded for a leg of mutton on the London docks.'

The Burmese is one of today's most popular breeds, especially in the USA where in 1989 three out of the top twenty cats were of that breed. But life has not always been easy for this cat in the USA. During its comparatively short time as a championship breed its status was once suspended for six years (see page 60); in the 1970s there was so much disagreement over the proposed introduction of the champagne and platinum colours that these had to be called Malayan; and attempts to produce cats with heads having shorter noses, rounder skulls and more prominent eyes resulted in many deformed kittens. Despite such setbacks the Burmese breed has survived and is now so popular that in the GCCF in Britain it has its own section at shows.

So great was the interest in the Burmese that it was not surprising that some enterprising breeder would want to add other colours to its range and that a black panther-like cat would be bred with Burmese as one of its ancestors (see page 62). Much later the breeding programme, involving matings between Silver Chinchilla Persian and Burmese in Britain, ultimately resulted in Burmese-shaped cats sans Burmese coat shading. This new variety was named Burmilla. It has inherited a large number of basic colour genes from the Burmese combined with tabby pattern genes, wide band genes and inhibitor genes from the Silver Chinchilla. As a result Burmillas are bred in solid colours and all colours and patterns of tabby.

In the southernmost area of South East Asia the feral and house cats are, as they were centuries ago, shorthairs with the warm climate form of the African wildcat or Indian desert cat. Blue cats were known to be particularly valued in Thailand (see page 70) and imports into the USA from 1959 onwards allowed for the evolution of the cat fancy Korat. The fierce protection given to the breed by its adherents has helped to retain many of its original characteristics but has also meant that it has become a breed with a limited gene pool and some degree of inbreeding.

The stubby tail so frequently occurring in cats of Singapore and Japan is very rare in Europe so that the introduction of the native Japanese cat – the Japanese Bobtail – to the list of cat fancy breeds resulted in a great deal of interest from breeders. Their inscrutable Oriental looks combined with their unusual tails (no two quite alike) and the attractive coat colours and patterns assured the breed of instant success. They are well known throughout the world in the form of the *Maneki–Neko* good luck porcelain or ceramic figures Using a cat for good luck may seem surprising in a country where folklore features cats as fierce creatures. There are tales of packs of cats tormenting entire villages and of dead mothers-in-law who are reincarnated as cats to haunt their families. However cats are also admired in Japan, both for their good manners and for their independence.

The Bengal was evolved in the 1960s from matings between leopard cats and domestics. But the truly man-made breeds of the group are the Snowshoe, which combines the pointed pattern of the Siamese with the hardiness and white markings of the American or European Shorthair; the Ocicat which evolved as a result of selective breeding from crosses between Abyssinian and Siamese; and the Havana which went on to become an Oriental breed in Europe but stopped short to become a sleek-bodied moderate type foreign breed in the USA.

The last cat of the group is the Sphynx – a controversial variety currently enjoying renewed popularity in the USA (see page 80). Whether the curious appearance of this breed compensates its owners for the fact that it has no silky coat to groom is uncertain. In fact the Sphynx do have a slight degree of coat and feel warm and soft the touch. All those coming into contact with them remark upon their wonderful personality. Phil Magitti, a writer for the USA *Cats* magazine, has commented:

A virulent form of the vapours affects some people the first time they visit a cat show. After a turn or two around the hall they sadly proclaim that Persians snuffle like bulldogs, Siamese look like strings and show cats in general are 'uncatlike'. . . . I am obliged to issue the following disclaimer. The Sphynx cat is indeed a real cat. It eats real food, sleeps real long, runs real good, purrs real loud and makes real use of its litterbox!

Grooming the Sphynx involves caring for its skin rather than for its coat. Regular washing to remove the skin secretions is recommended and owners are wise to use a mild Ph balanced shampoo when so doing. Grooming techniques for other breeds of the group vary. The Russian coat is often brushed in the opposite direction to the natural lie of the hair and then lightly tipped back into place in order to enhance the plushy effect; whereas grooming the Bombay and Burmese means polishing the close-lying coat until it shines.

Abyssinian

Name
Abyssinian (English); Abessinier (German); Abyssin (French). Named after Abyssinia (now Ethiopia). In its early days the breed was known variously as Spanish cat, probably because it had migrated on the trading ships that plied between Spain and Ceylon for many years; Russian cat, because it also travelled on trade routes from North India to Russia; Rabbit cat; Hare cat; Bunny cat and Cunny, probably because there is a superficial resemblance to the coat of a rabbit; British Tick; Ticked cat; or Abyssinian-type cat.

Origins
Said by Dr Gordon Staples in 1862 to trace its descent from a cat taken from Abyssinia to Britain as a gift for a Mrs Barrett-Leonard at the end of the Abyssinian War. Mrs Barrett-Leonard was the wife of one of a party of British troops sent to Abyssinia under the command of Sir Robert Napier to deal with an international incident arising from the arrest of a number of Europeans and the subsequent suicide of the Abyssinian Emperor. The cat's name is recorded as Zula, after the place where the troops landed. However, Harrison Weir, the instigator of the British cat fancy, believed the Abyssinian to be the result of selective breeding in Britain. Writing in 1889, he stated that a cross between an English wildcat and a domestic cat had produced kittens similar to those from Abyssinia. It is a recorded fact that more sinuous Asian-type cats would have been the norm in the region of Abyssinia. Gold Tick, one early Abyssinian, had a pedigree showing that her dam was a South African wildcat. Whatever the breed's origin, the coat pattern is undoubtedly due to mutation which occurred in Ceylon and/or the Bay of Bengal in ancient times.

Folklore
Known as 'the child of the Gods', the Abyssinian is considered by many to be the descendant of the sacred cats worshipped in the temples of Egypt *circa* 2,000–1,000 BC. The male cat represented the sun god Ra and the female cat represented the fertility goddess Bast.

Conformation
General build is moderately long and slender, neither stocky nor svelte, with an elegant head showing rounded contours generally, large alert ears and slightly slanting eyes. The tail, if measured alongside the body, would reach nearly to the shoulder.

Coat
Medium-length shorthair topcoat, lying fairly close to the body with each hair showing double or treble banding (ticking) of alternate light and dark with darker tips, and with shorter, softer undercoat of the lighter colour. Ears preferably tufted.

Colours
Ruddy; blue; chocolate; sorrel; lilac; fawn; red; cream; also tortie versions of these colours; silver versions; and tortie silver versions.

Patterns
Evenly ticked, sometimes with shading on the darker colour along the spine and always with the lighter colour, without ticking, on the underside, chest and inside legs. The tail is without the usual tabby rings but the tip is of the darker colour. Boots of the darker colour are apparent at the back of the hind legs. The usual tabby pattern is seen on the head with the characteristic tabby thumb marks on the ears. At moulting time the loss of topcoat combined with the fading of the tips of the old hairs sometimes produces an uneven appearance to the ticking. The undercoat varies in colour with the seasons and in some cats the undercoat is greyish.

Eyes
Gold or green in North America. Amber, green or yellow in most other cat fancy organizations, with the addition of hazel in one of the two British organizations.

Variation
The Abyssinian of North America developed to be slightly different from that of Britain, with a rounder muzzle and shorter head. In recent years the standards of Britain and Europe have been amended to avoid a pointed muzzle and to require more rounded contours in general. However, slight differences between the North American and the European-type Abyssinian remain. In North America only ruddy, blue and sorrel are recognized for show competition, and the sorrel variety is known as red. The ruddy variety is known as 'usual' in one cat fancy organization in Britain. The chocolate, lilac, red, cream and tortie varieties are recognized for competition only in Britain.

Personality
A rather highly-strung breed, cautious but devoted to its owners. Prefers to live as the only cat or in a very small cat family. Keen climber.

Voice
Quiet, even when 'calling'.

Kittens
Kittens are born with very dark tipping and a solid dark skullcap which breaks and disappears with maturity. Ticking does not show until the kitten is about two months old, first appearing on the tail and legs. The full beauty of the coat does not appear until the cat is nearly two years old.

Show Status
First recognized for championship competition in Britain in 1882 under the name 'Abyssinian-type'. First shown in the USA in 1909. Now shown as a championship breed worldwide but most popular in the USA.

Breeding
Only Abyssinians are allowed in Abyssinian pedigrees.

Usual (ruddy) Abyssinian

Bengal

Name
The name reflects the origins of the breed and was in common use to describe hybrids between domestic cats and *Felis bengalensis* (the leopard cat) for many years. When the sale of wild exotic cats in shops became illegal in the USA the name was retained as the name of the new breed under development from cats descending from such matings. It is under this name that the developing breed has been accepted for cat fancy competition. Formerly known as Leopardette. This name was the first choice of the original breeder and many breeders still prefer it.

Origins
Hybrids between domestic and small wildcats have been bred for at least a century and as early as 1871 such hybrids are on record in the English cat fancy. 'Hybrid wildcats' were among the winners at the 1871 Crystal Palace Show. Since then the list of wildcat species hybridized with domestic cats has lengthened to include the bobcat, the leopard cat, the jungle cat, the margay, the Indian desert cat, the European forest wildcat, the black-footed cat, the little spotted cat and the serval. But although many breeders were mating small wildcats to domestics in the 1960s and 1970s the Bengal breeding programme officially commenced in 1963 when Jean Sugden, who had graduated as a genetics student in the 1940s, mated a female Asian leopard cat imported from Malaysia to a male domestic cat adopted from a shelter. The single kitten was reared with a Himalayan (Colourpoint Persian) litter and cared for by the litter's dam. The kitten was named KinKin and was subsequently mated back to her sire, producing both spotted and solid-coloured kittens. For a while the breeding project was abandoned and not recommended until the late 1970s. Mrs Sugden (who by then had re-married and become Mrs Mill) obtained eight females from matings between Asian leopard cats and domestic shorthairs from Dr Willard Centerwall, a geneticist at the University of California. Additional domestic shorthair males were obtained as mates and the Bengal breeding programme was really under way. Although in the initial crosses the males proved to be sterile the breed as it has evolved is now fully fertile and, although the cats bear a striking resemblance to the leopard cat, they are now completely domestic in behaviour and habit.

Conformation
About the same size as a domestic cat but with a striking resemblance to the Asian leopard cat, with a long, thick and heavily-muscled body with strong legs and unusually large feet. Tail carried low. Head rather large in proportion to the body with small rounded ears and sometimes with slightly bulbous nostrils.

Coat
Of texture resembling a pelt rather than normal cat fur and resembling that of the wild Asian leopard cat.

Colours
Black on bright orange (leopard); black on rich mahogany (mink); brown on lighter orange (sorrel).

Patterns
A rosetted spot pattern with rosettes formed by partial circles of spots around a coloured centre. Single spotting also occurs. Underparts lighter.

Eyes
Yellow.

Variation
Clarity of spotting varies slightly when moulting.

Personality
Quick, agile and intelligent.

Voice
Often have a peculiar gravelly voice but usually non-vocal.

Kittens
Kittens have a somewhat coarse stand-up coat which tends to hide the spotting for the first three or four months. As the baby coat is moulted the true coat is grown. The rufous colouring may take nearly a year to reach its final richness.

Show Status
First exhibited in the 1980s in shows organized by TICA in the USA. Subsequently exhibited in France in 1988. Championship status not yet granted.

Breeding
Must have three or more generations of Bengal breeding.

Bombay

Name
The name was chosen to evoke the black leopard or panther of India, which inspired the creation of the breed.

Origins
Designed and first developed to resemble a small black leopard in the 1950s by an American breeder named Nikki Horner. Grand Champion Shawnee Anthracite, a black American Shorthair, was mated to Grand Champion Hill House Daniella, a sable Burmese, and several years of selection for Burmese breed type followed. The first champion was Kejo Kyrie, owned and bred by Pat Taylor in the USA. Although the breed first resembled both parent breeds it has evolved to become a black cat of Burmese type. The written standard is very similar to that for the Burmese, although there remain breeders who feel that the Bombay is a longer cat than the Burmese, with less nose break, longer legs and a longer, thinner tail. However Nikki Horner sees the cat as a Burmese with black fur. The Bombay is now also bred in Britain in programmes from Burmese and British Shorthairs and as a result of matings in the Burmilla breeding programmes. Just as the British-type Burmese varies from that of North America, so does the British Bombay vary from the American Bombay.

Conformation
A medium-size cat of moderate build, neither cobby nor tubular. Rounded head with wide-set, rather large eyes and a short, well-developed muzzle. The tail is medium in length.

Coat
Very short and satin-like, lying close to the body.

Colours
Dense, jet black.

Eyes
Deep gold, ranging to copper.

Variation
Eye colour may fade as the cat ages.

Personality
Dominant and assertive.

Voice
Very vocal.

Kittens
Young kittens may have shadowy tabby markings in the coat. Eye colour develops slowly from baby blue through grey to gold or copper.

Show Status
Accepted for championship competition in the USA by the CFF in 1976 and subsequently by TICA and the ACFA. Also accepted for competition without championship status in other US associations and in the CA of Britain and the clubs of FIFe.

Breeding
Varies with the registering association. Allowable outcross breeds in the USA are Black American Shorthair and Sable Burmese.

Burmese

Name

Burmese (English and French); Burma (German). Named after Burma, where the founder cat of the breed originated. Some breeders in the USA refer to their cats as Traditional Burmese, retaining the Burmese breed name for the heavier, flatter-faced variety.

Origins

A well-documented breed, the Burmese evolved from a cat named Wong Mau who was taken to the USA from Burma in 1930 by Dr Thompson, a former US navy ship's doctor. When he acquired Wong Mau he was practising psychiatry in San Francisco, where he also bred cats – 'Mau' being his cattery name. Wong Mau was of Malay type and was originally considered to be a dark Siamese; but Thompson realized that there was a difference. In collaboration with breeder and geneticist friends he set out to determine her genotype. The results of the breeding tests showed Wong Mau to be a hybrid with a new dark-coated breed of cat which, because of Wong Mau's original home, was called Burmese. In 1942 three more cats from Burma were taken to the west coast of the USA, but only one of them appears in early Burmese pedigrees. The first breed standards described a cat of foreign, muscular type; and although the required colour was brown there was a variety of shades. Eventually the rich dark brown (slightly lighter on the stomach and slightly darker on the head) was established. The first Burmese were sent to Britain in 1949 to Sydney and Lilian France, who were already well-known as breeders of Siamese, and in 1955 a daughter of one of the original imports produced a blue kitten. While American breeders then concentrated on the elimination of bars and points in the sable brown, British breeders then outcrossed to develop a wider range of colours.

In the 1970s a new-look Burmese appeared in the USA with a shorter nose and muzzle and a rounder head. The line responsible for this look unfortunately carried deleterious genes which led to serious malformations and vigorous attempts have been made by breeders to eradicate these problems. In general the American standard describes a much cobbier, heavier cat, but European breeders who based their standards on the original take the view that the Burmese, as a cat of Far Eastern origin, should remain a cat of definite foreign type and continue to develop their Burmese in that direction.

Folklore

Described in the Thai *Cat Book* poems as the *Su-pa-lak* or *Thong Daeng*, a cat which protects its owners from danger, saves them from evil and brings them happiness. The translation of the verses is:

> Of magnificent appearance with shape the best,
> Coloured like copper, this cat is beautiful:
> The light of her eyes is as a shining ray.

Conformation

Of muscular, athletic build, shorter-faced and more stocky in the USA than in Europe, although all breed standards require a rounded head with considerable breadth between the eyes, and a short muzzle. Ears are set well apart on a slightly domed skull. The tail, which should be slender and of medium length, tapers slightly to a blunt tip.

Coat

Very short and like satin, shading to a lighter colour on the underparts.

Colours and Patterns

Brown (sable in USA); blue; chocolate (champagne in USA); lilac (platinum in USA); red; cream; black tortoiseshell; blue tortoiseshell; chocolate tortoiseshell; lilac tortoiseshell. Only the first four colours are recognized in the USA. Burmese-type cats with white coats are bred in the UK and Australia but are not considered to be true Burmese as the characteristic Burmese slightly shaded coat is masked by white. These cats are related to Burmese in the same way as Foreign Whites are related to Siamese.

Eyes

Yellow to gold.

Variation

All colours darken with age and shading becomes less apparent. Eye colour tends to fade in older cats, particularly in blues.

Personality

Renowned for its rumbustious, somewhat highly-strung nature.

Voice

Has a very strong voice and may be noisy unless neutered.

Kittens

Brown/sable Burmese kittens are born *café-au-lait* coloured and darken gradually over the first few months of life. New-born Burmese of other colours are born similarly pale. Eye colour develops from kitten blue through grey-green to yellow or gold, but the rate of colour change varies between Burmese colours and in blues a slight hint of green is acceptable. Some cats retain a definite greenish tint and this is regarded as a fault.

Show Status

First recognized in the USA by CFA in 1936. Championship status withdrawn by CFA in 1947 because of difficulties in classification between the true Burmese and the hybrid (now Tonkinese) kittens. Championship status in the CFA restored in 1953. Now a championship breed worldwide.

Breeding

Only Burmese are allowed in Burmese pedigrees.

Brown (sable) Burmese

Burmilla

Name
Chosen by the originator of the breed to recall the two parent breeds, Burmese and Chinchilla Persian. In the GCCF of Britain it is known as Tipped Silver of Burmese type.

Origins
Evolved from progeny of an accidental mating in north London between a lilac Burmese, Bambino Lilac Fabergé, and a silver Chinchilla Persian, Jemari Sanquist. Both cats were owned by the Baroness Miranda von Kirchberg, whose cattery name is Astahazy. She was immediately impressed by the vitality and potential beauty of the resultant silver litter which was born on 11 September 1981. She made plans for a programme of backcrossing to Burmese, based on the knowledge that the silver colour is inherited as a dominant and the opinion that shading and tipping is inherited as a semi-dominant. This programme was designed to perfect a Burmese type and to avoid inbreeding by the use of a number of different Burmese pedigree lines. The goal agreed was a shorthair cat of Burmese character and conformation with the tipped coat pattern of the silver Chinchilla Persian.

Subsequently a group of breeders led by Charles and Thérèse Clarke of the Kartush cattery in Wantage, Oxfordshire, formed a breed club and formulated a programme of inbreeding designed to preserve the dense coat and to perfect the silver tipping. This programme was commenced with the half-brother-and-sister Astahazy Gemma (registered in the CA as Gemma of Kartush) and Astahazy Jacynth (registered in the CA as Jacynth of Kartush). By 1984 there were two main breeding programmes, two breed clubs and two registering bodies. The original breeding programme was producing ever-improving Burmese type but a lower number of tipped coats while the second breeding programme was producing ever-improving tipped coats but lower numbers of cats showing improvement towards the desired Burmese type. Both groups now recognize the advantages of each other's breeding methods and both continue to work to the original aim of a shorthair cat of Burmese type with the shaded or tipped colouring. The fact that breeding has gone in different directions in each group now provides opportunity for them each to outcross to the other in order to improve the characteristics of both.

Conformation
Of muscular build, just like the Burmese, and with the typical domed head, ear set and eye shape of the Burmese. The tail, which should be slender and of medium length, tapers slightly to a blunt tip. While still developing as a breed, many Burmillas tend to have over-large rounded eyes and rather short thick tails. Breeders aim to correct these faults before championship recognition is sought.

Coat
Short and soft in texture, though while a developing breed many cats have over-long coats with woolly undercoat. This is a fault.

Colours
Black silver; sepia silver; blue silver; chocolate silver; lilac silver; red silver; cream silver; all colours of tortie silver; black golden; sepia golden; blue golden; chocolate golden; lilac golden; all colours of tortie golden.

Patterns
Golden or silver coat shaded or tipped with the basic colour.

Eyes
Green or blue-green.

Variation
Eye colour may fade with age. The colour of the shading or tipping may darken with age. The degree of shading or tipping may change with age.

Personality
Sweet-natured and affectionate. Slightly quieter in habit than its parent breed of Burmese.

Voice
Strong yet melodious.

Kittens
Kittens inheriting the Burmese pattern along with the tipped or shaded coat will be born much lighter than their littermates but will darken as they mature. Eye colour in young kittens is blue, changing to green as the kitten develops. In all kittens the degree of heavily pigmented hair will be greater than in the adult cat.

Show Status
First exhibited in 1983 at a show organized by the CA of Britain. Accepted as a provisional breed of the CA of Great Britain in 1984. Eligible for competition as a new breed in all countries of FIFe.

Breeding
While still a provisional breed, both parent breeds may be present within three generations; but breeders of the CA of Britain allow pedigrees including only Burmese and Burmilla. In the GCCF breeding policy allows for the re-introduction of silver Chinchilla Persian if necessary.

Egyptian Mau

Name
The name is derived from the African wildcat, also known locally as the Egyptian Cat. The word *mau* simply means cat.

Origins
First recorded in Italy in the early 1950s when Princess Natalie Troubetskoy, a Russian exile living in Rome, saw and wanted to purchase a smoke male and a spayed silver female of Egyptian Mau type. They were not for sale, but she was able to purchase a similar female cat in Cairo. Named Baba, she was mated to the Italian smoke male Geppa and bore two bronze kittens named Joseph and Jude. Baba was later mated to her son and produced a second female. In 1956 Princess Troubetskoy moved to the USA where the cats were registered with CFF. The development of the breed has been almost entirely in the USA.

Folklore
Considered to be a direct descendant of the larger African wildcat, *Felis silvestris lybica*, which was domesticated, then deified, by the ancient Egyptians and subsequently taken from Egypt to Italy by the Romans. Immortalized in the *Book of the Dead*, which portrays the Egyptian Mau as Ra, the sun god, slaying a serpent, and as the living form of the goddess Bast, the Egyptian cat-goddess, representative of the moon, the Sun god's eye during the night.

Conformation
General build is midway between the stocky British/American/European Shorthairs and the Orientals. The head is a slightly rounded wedge, with upstanding, slightly pointed ears, towards which the large eyes are gently slanted. The slightly tapered tail, if measured along the length of the cat, reaches the shoulder where it meets the back.

Coat
Medium length, dense and resilient to the touch, and long enough to show two or more bands of ticking in the bronze and smoke varieties. In these the individual hairs are banded, and have black tips. In the smoke variety the hairs are light at the roots shading to black tips, but with no ticking.

Colours
Silver (black pattern on silver); bronze (black pattern on bronze); smoke (black pattern on ashy silver).

Patterns
The typical spotted tabby pattern of domestic cats, with clear spots made up of non-agouti hair evenly spaced on an agouti ground colour, except in the smoke where the ground is simply a lighter colour of non-agouti hair. Spots may vary in size and shape, but must be distinct.

Eyes
Gooseberry green.

Variation
Spots lose distinction at the time of the moult and the topcoat may become rusty in some colours. Eye colour fades with age.

Personality
Slightly shy of strangers, but very loving to its owners. Sociable with other cats of its own breed but selective in its choice of close companion amongst cats of other breeds. Very active and lively. Easily trained.

Voice
Much quieter than Orientals.

Kittens
Kittens are born with the spotted pattern, although it is darker and blurred. In smokes the full colour effect will not be apparent until the cat is about two years of age. Eye colour develops slowly from kitten blue through grey to green, although some cats have eyes with an amber cast which may persist until they are eighteen months old.

Show Status
First exhibited in the mid-1950s at the International Cat Show in Rome, and subsequently at the Empire Cat Show in the USA in 1957. Championship status granted in the USA in 1968. Also exhibited in Canada, Japan and some independent show cat organizations in Europe.

Breeding
Only Egyptian Mau allowed in pedigrees.

Havana Brown

Name
Named by its originators to evoke the colour of Havana cigars. The term havana is also used by Oriental breeders to describe solid chocolate colour. In the early days of the breed it was also known as Swiss Mountain cat, Berkshire or Reading Brown, and in Britain Chestnut Brown Foreign.

Origins
The first mention of solid-coated brown cats is in the Thai *Cat Book* poems, but it is not clear whether the cat referred to is the Havana or the Burmese. A brown cat was exhibited in 1894 as 'Swiss Mountain cat', but there was little interest in the cat fancy. Mrs Cox Ife, a prominent cat fancier of her time, wrote in 1939: 'In the early days of the breed many chocolate-coloured Siamese appeared on the show bench – that is chocolate-coloured all over.' The fact that black kittens were reportedly bred from brown parents makes it clear that both solid brown and Burmese brown as well as the Siamese/Burmese hybrids now known as Tonkinese were bred, and that fanciers could not distinguish between them. The Havana Brown of today owes its existence to Mrs Monro-Smith, the Baroness E. von Ullman, Mrs Armitage Hargreaves and Mrs Elsie Fisher, all of whom started breeding programmes in the early 1950s.

Baroness von Ullman eventually obtained Craigiehilloch Bronze Wing, a Havana bred by Mrs Dora Clarke and sired by Elmtower Bronze Idol from Mrs Monro-Smith's independent breeding programme, and a breeders' group was formed. When the breed was finally recognized in Britain the name Havana was objected to, on the grounds that cats might be bred for their pelts just as were Havana rabbits. The name chosen to replace Havana was Chestnut Brown Foreign.

The first show standard followed that of the Russian Blue, except that the colour was described as 'rich brown, even and sound'. Particular mention was made of the fact that exaggerated length of head would be penalized and that the type was that of all foreign breeds. In 1954 the combination of the newly introduced chocolate into pedigrees which carried blue as a result of the founder breed of Russian Blue resulted in the birth of a lilac or lavender-coated cat called Praha Allegro Agitato. The breeder was Mrs Elsie Fisher.

The first Havanas to reach the USA were Laurentide Brown Pilgrim and Roofspringer Mahogany. Roofspringer Marguerite, litter sister to Mahogany, was bought by the wife of an American serviceman with a view to mating her in Britain before going back to the USA.

The breed was enthusiastically taken up by US breeders and judges who worked hard to develop the type and coat described in the original standard. Exports from Britain of lilacs, to be known in the USA as lavenders, were made by Mrs Elsie Fisher, and that colour became a variety with the same conformation. But in Britain exhibitors were hampered by disagreement. Articles appearing in the cat press likening the breed conformation to that of the Russian were followed by others which stated the Chestnut Brown Group's intention to work towards Siamese type.

Eventually those advocating Siamese type won the day in Britain and outcrosses to Siamese became the norm. From that point the Havana of Britain and the Havana Brown of the USA and Canada became and have remained effectively two different breeds. The British Havana is now a member of the Oriental Shorthair group and the name is retained to describe its colour. The Havana of the USA, Canada and Japan is nearer the original concept of the breed although it has its own characteristics which are distinctively different from both the Russian and the Siamese.

Conformation
A breed of medium size and body length with slender legs and a tail which reaches just short of the shoulder. The head is longer than it is wide and narrows slightly to a rounded muzzle. Seen from the side the nose has a definite break in direction at the level of the eyes. Ears are large and set wide but not flaring.

Coat
Medium length and smooth.

Colours
Mahogany brown.

Eyes
Chartreuse.

Personality
Intelligent and desirous of human attention and companionship.

Voice
Not very vocal.

Kittens
Kittens are born with brown coats but the glossy look with reddish highlights may not be fully developed until about six months. Eye colour develops gradually from kitten blue.

Show Status
First exhibited in London in 1953. Championship status granted in Britain in 1958. Championship status followed in the USA by the UCF and the breed was first shown in championship classes at its Siamese Society show in 1959. Now a championship breed as Havana Brown in USA, Canada and Japan. In Britain the breed is no longer seen in its original form but the name Havana has been retained for the chocolate-coloured Oriental Shorthair.

Breeding
Only Havana Brown allowed in pedigrees.

Japanese Bobtail

Name
The name reflects its country of origin and characteristic bobbed tail.

Origins
Charles Darwin recorded a high incidence of cats with short kinky tails throughout 'the Malayan archipelago, Siam, Pegu and Burmah'. More recently, studies of cat populations have revealed that stubby-tailed cats, though very common in Singapore, are rare in Europe; and geneticists now believe that the Bobtail indicates that all the cats of South-East Asia descend from a small number of individuals taken into the region thousands of years ago. The domestic cat is thought to have arrived in Japan from Korea or China in the seventh, eighth or ninth century, and the first written record of cats in Japan is a Japanese novel by the tutor-governess to the Japanese Empress of more than 1,000 years ago. No mention is made of tail structure, all descriptions being confined to coat markings and colours. Over the centuries the Japanese Bobtail established itself as the *Kazoku Neko* (family cat) of Japan, and geneticists believe that the bobtail characteristic first mutated there and spread to other parts of Asia. Such cats are mentioned in the medieval Thai *Cat Book* poems. By 1963 the Japanese had started to establish their own cat fancy and when judges from the USA were invited to a Japanese cat show they were most captivated by the Japanese Neko (cat). The Japanese realized that the cats they had thought of as household pets were unique and began, at last, to take them seriously. The Japanese Bobtail was first protectively bred in Japan itself by Judy Crawford, the wife of a US serviceman stationed in Japan after the Second World War. Subsequently a pet Bobtail taken to the USA by a returning serviceman was seen by a breeder named Elizabeth Freret, who imported cats from Judy Crawford to start the US breeding programme in 1968. Soon after this Judy Crawford returned to the USA herself, taking thirty-eight Japanese Bobtails with her. From that time development of pedigree strains continued in both countries.

Folklore
The first cats to step on Japanese soil are said to have been black. These were followed by whites and then, when orange (red) cats arrived from South-East Asia, the Mi-ke (tortie and white) was born. Mi-ke means 'three fur' – referring to the three colours of red, black and white. Considered to be a cat of good fortune, the Japanese cat is often depicted wearing the good-luck colour of *mi-ke* (tortoiseshell and white) and with one forefoot raised. Such cat statues are known as welcome cats or *Maneki-Neko*. Bobtailed orange cats are mentioned also in the Thai *Cat Book* poems with the legend that if you found such a cat on your doorstep on New Year's Day the coming year would be a lucky one.

Conformation
A medium-sized cat with a slender though well-muscled body, long slender legs and a short variably kinked or curved tail held high with the hair often fanning out to create a pom-pom appearance. It has high cheek-bones with eyes set in an Asian slant which, together with the long nose, combine to produce a distinct Japanese look, especially in profile.

Coat
Medium length, fairly flat-lying and without any discernible undercoat.

Colours
Japan's traditional *mi-ke* (tortie and white) colouring of black, red and white is preferred but white, black, red, black and white, red and white and tortoiseshell are also popular and virtually any other colour is accepted for exhibition.

Patterns
All patterns and combination of patterns other than Abyssinian ticked tabby and Siamese coat pattern.

Eyes
Any eye colour which harmonizes with the coat colour including blue, yellow or even odd eyes in white or nearly all white cats.

Variation
Some coat colours show rusty shadings just prior to the moult or shadowy markings in kittenhood and adolescence. Whites may have coloured smudges on the head until the first or second moult.

Personality
The Bobtail has an outgoing nature and, while mixing well with other breeds, prefers its own kind.

Voice
Has a wide range of chirps and miaows and is vocal without being noisy.

Kittens
Eye colour develops from kitten blue to a colour in accordance with the coat colour.

Show Status
Accepted for registration in the CFA of the USA in 1969, followed by provisional status in 1971 and championship status in 1976. Accepted with provisional status by the CA of Britain in 1986 and for championship status by the countries in FIFe in 1988.

Breeding
Only Japanese Bobtails are allowed in Japanese Bobtail pedigrees.

Korat

Name
The name is derived from its place of origin in Korat, the north-eastern province of Thailand, and is said to have been first given by King Chulalongkorn. Known in Thailand by its original Thai name of Si-Sawat.

Origins
The Korat is a breed that evolved naturally and cat fanciers have sought to preserve it in its natural form by disallowing outcrosses to other breeds. First recorded in the medieval Thai *Cat Book* poems, from which pictures of Korats were subsequently copied and included in the Smud Koi papyrus, produced during the reign of King Rama V in the late nineteenth century. In 1947 Jean Johnson of the USA saw Korats while searching Thailand for Siamese cats. She was told that the Si-Sawat (Korat) was the true Thai cat and in 1959 she was able to obtain a pair from a queen named Mom Noel who was born in Korat and owned by Mme Ruen Abhibal Rajamaitri of Bangkok. The kittens were named Nara and Darra and in 1962 they were joined in the USA by Mahajaya Dok Rak, Nai Sri Sawat Miow and Me Luk from the Cholburi Province. Other Korats followed and a breeding programme was started. In 1965 the first breed standard was compiled.

Folklore
Described in the *Cat Book* poems as having been created by two skilled hermits. Those who bring good luck being credited to Ka-la-i-ko-te and those of good pedigree to Eyes-of-fire. Considered to bring good luck to their owners, Korats are often given as marriage gifts in Thailand. They are also said to have been used in rain-making ceremonies in ancient Thailand.

Conformation
Medium in size with a muscular body, a characteristic heart-shaped head and large, luminous eyes. The slightly tapering tail, if measured along the length of the cat, reaches the point of the shoulder so that the distance from the nape of the neck to the root of the tail is equal to the distance from the root of the tail to the ground.

Coat
Short to medium-short, even-toned blue fur with pale silvery tips which give a sheen to the entire coat.

Colours and Patterns
Blue with silver tipping.

Eyes
Luminous green in adults, yellow to amber-green in kittens and adolescents.

Variation
Old hair may take on a brownish tinge during the moult.

Personality
Playful and intelligent.

Voice
Pretty, rather quiet voice.

Kittens
Coat and eye colour develops very slowly so that some Korats do not attain full perfection until they are several years old.

Show Status
First presented in 1965 and first exhibited as a championship breed at the ACA King of Prussia Show in Pennsylvania, USA. Granted championship status by CFA and Crown in 1969 and recognized in Canada the same year. Recognized in South Africa in 1968 and in Britain in 1975 (though without championship status). Now recognized for championships worldwide.

Breeding
Only Korats are allowed in Korat pedigrees.

Ocicat

Name
The name was chosen as an amalgam of 'ocelette' and 'accicat', two names first considered – the former because the cats resemble small ocelots and the latter because the first kitten was an accident. Ocelette and Accicat were used in the first year of the breed.

Origins
The first Ocicat was Dalai Tonga, bred in 1964 by Virginia Daly of Michigan, USA, as a result of an accidental mating between a champion, Whitehead Elegante Sun, a chocolate point Siamese, and a hybrid queen named Dalai She. The queen was from a breeding programme for Abyssinian tabby point Siamese and had an Abyssinian dam, champion Dalai Deta Tim of Selene and a seal point Siamese sire, Dalai Tomby Platter. After reading an article on the African wildcat, *Felis silvestris lybica* by the geneticist Dr Clyde Keeler, Mrs Daly repeated the mating and, by so doing, produced the foundation stock for the Ocicat breed. With the birth of Dalai Talua the cinnamon colour was first seen in the breed although, at the time of Talua's birth, her colour was known as 'light chestnut' rather than cinnamon. The breed was then taken up by Tom Brown, who bred five generations of Ocicats' but his programme came to an end in about 1970. Despite a slow beginning breeders persisted in their efforts to develop the Ocicat as a breed and outcrosses to American Shorthair were made to increase size and to introduce the silver colours. Breeding programmes for the production of Ocicats were commenced in Europe when Karen Dupuis of West Germany started a new line with cats bred by Mrs M. Toreau. In 1984 she bred the first European Ocicat, named Tschi Miao Nadir. Later Karen Dupuis bred Tschi Miao Karam, a tawny Ocicat, from a mating between a chocolate Oriental and a red ticked tabby of Abyssinian and Siamese pedigree. Tschi Miao Karam subsequently became the first Ocicat to win international championship status.

Conformation
A large cat of moderate type, neither svelte nor cobby. Its head has gentle curves with a well-defined, slightly square muzzle. Legs are well-muscled and of medium length and the long tail tapers slightly towards the tip.

Coat
Fine-textured coat with a lustrous sheen and long enough to show definite agouti colour bands.

Colours
Tawny; chocolate; cinnamon; blue; lavender; fawn; also silver versions of these colours. Varieties without the spotted tabby pattern are also bred but are registered as Any Other Variety.

Patterns
Tabby tracing on the head and face with an 'M' mark on the centre forehead. Rows of round spots running along the spine. Spots scattered across the shoulders, hindquarters and on the torso.

Eyes
All eye colours, except blue.

Variation
Eye colour may fade with age. Spot clarity may lessen at the time of the moult.

Personality
Sweet-natured and affectionate, although not always happy in a large cat family.

Voice
Moderately quiet.

Kittens
Kittens are born with their spotted pattern but the general colouration appears darker and the pattern blurred until about the age of five weeks.

Show Status
First exhibited in the USA. Championship status granted in the USA in 1987. First shown in Europe at Dijon, France, when the breed was accepted for championship competition by the independent clubs of Europe. Shown in the USA, Canada, Japan, Germany, France and Britain.

Breeding
Outcrosses to Abyssinians allowed until 1 January 1995, after which time only Ocicats will be allowed in Ocicat pedigrees.

Russian

Name

Russian (English); Russe (French); Russisch (German). The name is derived from the cat's supposed origin in the White Sea port of Arkhangel in the USSR. Most countries recognize blues only and use the word blue (bleu or blau) as part of the breed name. In the past a variety of names was used, including Spanish Blue; Archangel; Maltese; and Foreign Blue.

Origins

First recorded by Harrison Weir in 1899 as the Arkhangel Cat and later by others under a variety of names, the Russian is believed to have its origins among cats taken by merchant ships from the port of Arkhangel in the USSR to Sweden and thence to Western Europe. However the history is rather clouded by the fact that blue cats were also imported from the north of Norway and that these cats included some that were blue tabby. One of the pioneer breeders was Mrs Carew-Cox, who imported cats directly from Arkhangel to Britain at the end of the eighteenth century. Among these were a female known as Lingpopo and a male named King Vladimir, later to become sire of the famous Russian Blue stud Bayard. At the early cat shows all blue shorthair cats competed together, whether they were solid blue or tabby or of Russian or British in type, and it was not until 1912 that separation was achieved so that the Russians had a class named Foreign Blue. Breeders managed to get the original name of 'Russian' restored in 1939. After the war, in the Scandinavian countries a breeding programme commenced with matings between a blue cat from Finland called Pierette and a Siamese male named Longfellow of Annam. In Britain Russians were mated to blue point Siamese in an attempt to increase numbers and widen the gene pool. Not unexpectedly the Russian Blue began to develop towards a more Oriental-type cat, but over the last twenty-five years strenuous efforts have been made in Europe to re-create the breed as it was prior to the Second World War.

In the USA and Canada the Russian Blue is said to have first arrived around 1888–90 and the records show that Mrs Clinton Locke imported Lockehaven Royal Blue from a British breeder. The breed suffered from confusion between it and blue American Shorthairs (then known as Domestics) until the post-war European lines were imported to form the basis of a breeding programme towards the Russian as it is today. However there are still significant differences in the requirements for Russian Blues in North America and Europe. In Australasia the Russians are similar to those of Europe, although some legislating bodies in the Australian cat fancy recognize white Russian. In the UK only the Russian Blue has championship status but whites and blacks may also compete in non-championship classes.

Folklore

Said to derive from northern Russia, where its fur was prized by trappers for its beautiful colour and warmth. It is believed that this fur, with its outer coat of tough guard hairs and undercoat of water-resistant down hairs, served as protection in the semi-arctic areas of northern Russia. Popular legend has it that the Russian Blues travelled to Britain with the Vikings.

Conformation

In Europe the Russian is now a cat of moderate foreign type with medium limbs and a head shape specific to the breed with its short, wedged muzzle, tall upright ears which are very thin and sparsely furnished with hair and prominent whisker pads. The medium-long tail tapers towards the tip and reaches a point between the base of the rib-cage and the shoulder.

Coat

Medium-short, thick, plushy and upstanding, resembling the coat of a seal. In blues the coat has a silvery sheen. In whites the coat appears opaque and in blacks the coat is dense black with a decided sparkle. The unique coat – sometimes described as a double coat – is the reason for the characteristic differences between it and coats of other breeds with similar colour.

Colours

Blue. White and black also bred in some countries.

Eyes

Vivid green.

Variation

Coat texture varies with environment and time of year. Eye colour fades with age.

Personality

A sweet, rather pensive personality, usually rather shy with strangers yet affectionate to other cats and people they know.

Voice

Quieter than other Foreign Shorthair breeds.

Kittens

Kittens are born with blue coats, but the tone of blue may change with growth and shadowy tabby markings may be present in infancy. Eye colour develops slowly from kitten blue. Any hint of blue or yellow in the eyes or shadowy markings in the coat once the cat is adult are considered to be serious faults.

Show Status

First exhibited in Britain in 1880. Championship status now worldwide including the USSR, whose cat fancy is in its infancy and whose breeders now hope to re-establish the Russian Blue by imports.

Breeding

Only Russians are allowed in Russian pedigrees.

Singapura

Name
The name derives from the Malaysian name for Singapore. Alleged by the original breeders to have been known locally in Singapore as 'drain cats'.

Origins
Development as an exhibition breed is asserted to have resulted from conversations between a British pilot and his wife who were members of the Singapore Feline Society and Tommy Meadows, a former judge with the American CFF then living in Singapore. It is reported that the British couple described small ticked tabby cats as 'drain cats of Singapore'. The Meadows have stated that in 1974 they acquired a ticked tabby kitten, said to be an authentic 'drain cat', which they named Pusse, and that later they acquired a male and female. The female, Tes, and the male, Tickle, sired a litter of kittens to Pusse while the Meadows were still living in Singapore. In 1975 the Meadows left Singapore to return to the USA and took with them five of the ticked cats – Pusse, Tes, Tickle, Gladys and George, the latter two being the result of the mating between Pusse and Tickle. Once their future as an exhibition breed was considered the cats were named Singapura. In 1980 an American cat breeder holidaying in Singapore obtained another similar cat from a rescue organization there and this cat, together with the five owned by Hal and Tommy Meadows, were the founders of the original Singapura breed in the USA. Breeding undertaken demonstrated that some of the original cats carried the non-agouti gene which produces Burmese-coloured brown coats, and those working to develop the breed are attempting to eradicate this while perfecting the other characteristics. Recently new imports of cats, officially authenticated as the Singapura, have been made into the USA. Singapura have been derived from documented crosses between Abyssinian and Burmese, but some USA breeders maintain that the true Singapura owes its existence to feral cats of Singapore.

Folklore
Said to have originated from small cats living in the drains of Singapore. Although this story may be true there is only hearsay to support it, and virtually identical cats may be bred through crosses of Burmese and Abyssinian.

Conformation
A small, compact and solidly-muscled cat with strong legs, small feet and a blunt-tipped tapering tail which, if measured along the side of the cat, reaches nearly, but not quite, to the shoulder. The head is rounded with a medium-length muzzle and large eyes and ears. Required by some registering associations to weigh no more than six pounds, although adequate nutrition in the breed's new home in the USA has resulted in some cats which weigh appreciably more.

Coat
Very short, silky and close lying.

Colours
Sable brown ticked with warm ivory, with the muzzle, chin and chest the colour of unbleached muslin.

Patterns
Ticked throughout the body with the tips of the hair brown. Muzzle, chin, chest and stomach lighter. Tail tip solid brown. There are bars on the inside of the legs and brown spurs up the back of the hind legs.

Eyes
Hazel, green or yellow.

Variation
Kittens sometimes lack ticking and, when present, it may be unevenly distributed. Grey roots may occur in some parts of the coat during adolescence and at certain times of the year thereafter.

Personality
Active, inquisitive, intelligent and unafraid.

Voice
Fairly vocal.

Kittens
Kittens are born with blue eyes which develop towards hazel, yellow or green from about the age of nine weeks. Kitten coats may be slightly longer than in the adult.

Show Status
First exhibited in the late 1970s in the new breed and colour class in an ACFA show in the USA. Recognized for championship competition in the USA in 1979. May be exhibited for competition, but not for championships, in the CA of Britain and other European cat organizations.

Breeding
Only Singapuras are allowed in Singapura pedigrees in the USA. In countries where the breed has pedigrees tracing back to Abyssinians and Burmese these two breeds may be present.

Snowshoe

Name
Named by the original breeder to indicate that the breed has white markings in the form of boots.

Origins
Although white-marked cats with Siamese pattern had occasionally been bred as a result of accidental matings, the Snowshoe was the brainchild of Dorothy Hinds-Daugherty, a Siamese breeder who owned the Kensing cattery in Philadelphia, USA, in the 1960s. Early reports describe the Snowshoe as a variety that originated from matings between Siamese, but the known genetics of the breed make it clear that a cat with white markings must be among its ancestors. The antagonism of Siamese breeders to the Snowshoe in its early days was occasioned by the mistaken belief that white boots might become common in the Siamese breed if the new Snowshoe breed was allowed to continue. Another problem was the widely held belief that Snowshoes were a short-haired variety of Birman.

One Snowshoe breeder who persisted in her efforts was Vikki Olander of the Fur-Lo cattery in Norfolk, Virginia. She wrote the first breed standard and worked to obtain registration status in the CFA. By 1977 she was the only Snowshoe breeder left in the USA and possibly in the world.

In 1978 Jim Hoffman of the Sujym and Tadluk cattery in Defiance, Ohio, and Georgia Kuhnell contacted Vikki Olander. Together they revised the breed standard and set about recruiting additional breeders so that by 1986 there were fifteen breeders in the USA and one in Canada. The first champions attained their titles at the same time in May 1983 – both bred by Jim Hoffman, they were Champion Sujym Caribu of Katskeep and Champion Sujym Alaskan Sky.

In Britain a Snowshoe breeding programme was initiated after Patricia Turner of the Scintilla cattery in Britain saw Snowshoes while judging at an international show at the Madison Square Garden, New York. She noticed that they were very similar to cats she had bred as part of a genetic investigation into piebald white spotting. She contacted the US breed club for information and as a result a British breed club was formed and a number of breeders joined together in a Snowshoe breeding project. The founder breeders in Britain were Patricia Turner, her husband John Mais of the Jamais cattery, Pauline and Derek Parsons of the Shalimar cattery, both in Buckinghamshire, and Maureen Trompetto of the Lincret cattery Surrey.

Conformation
Medium to large with medium thickness of bone and well muscled throughout. The head and ears when seen from the front fit into an imaginary equilateral triangle with a medium-length muzzle. Eyes are shaped like walnuts, neither round nor oriental.

Coat
Fairly short, glossy but not fine-textured.

Colours
Seal and white point; blue and white point; chocolate and white point; lilac and white point; caramel and white point; red and white point; cream and white point; also the tortie versions of these colours; and the tabby versions. *Note:* only seal and white and blue and white are accepted for competition in the CFF.

Patterns
The Snowshoe pattern is complex, with the white markings superimposed on the basic Siamese pattern. The white areas on a perfectly-marked Snowshoe are a white inverted 'V' on the muzzle and extending to the bridge of the nose with a thin line of white, the thinner the better, underneath the chin and extending down the chest and along the underbelly. On the front legs are white ankle-high boots and on its hind legs there are white boots reaching a point just below the hock joints.

Eyes
Brilliant blue.

Variation
The coat, other than in the white areas, darkens with age and with exposure to cold. The darkest areas (the points) may brindle or become bleached by brilliant sunlight, especially in chocolate and white points.

Personality
Widely described as bomb-proof, the Snowshoe is a happy-go-lucky breed and shows great affection to its owners.

Voice
Variable. Some Snowshoes have strident voices while others make no more than a hardly-heard squeak. As a hybrid breed some Snowshoes have the voice of their Siamese ancestors while others give a clue to their American or European Shorthair roots.

Kittens
Kittens are born white or nearly white and the points colour and markings only become evident as the kitten develops. In very pale varieties the actual degree of pattern may not be evident until the cat is nearly two years old.

Show Status
Championship status in CFF of the USA granted in 1982. Shown as a new breed, without championship status in TICA, ACA and ACFA. Accepted as a provisional breed, without championship status, by the CA of Britain in 1986. Eligible for unrecognized breed classes in all twenty-seven countries of FIFe and as a new breed in the independent cat associations of Europe.

Breeding
In the USA pedigrees may include Snowshoes, Siamese and Bi-coloured American or Oriental Shorthair. In Britain pedigrees may also include Bi-coloured British or European Shorthair.

Chocolate and white point Snowshoe

Sphynx

Name

Said to be so named because early breeders felt that there was a similarity between their cats and the Egyptian cat sculptures in the British Museum and the Louvre. Also known as the Canadian Hairless Cat. The first recorded hairless cats were known as Mexican Hairless Cats.

Origins

Hairless cats were first recorded by Mr F. J. Shinick of Alburquerque, New Mexico. In a letter printed in the 1903 *Book of the Cat* he stated that he had obtained two hairless cats from Indians living a few miles away from his home. Reports of others were made sporadically from countries including Australia, France and Morocco. In 1938 the geneticist Professor E. Letard reported on hairless Siamese cats in France. Then in 1966 a male hairless kitten was born to a black and white domestic pet named Elizabeth in Ontario, Canada. The kitten was so unusual that a Siamese breeder resolved to attempt development of hairless cats as a new breed under the name of Sphynx. She obtained the kitten and its mother and mated them together. The resultant litter was of both hairless and normal kittens. CFA gave the breed provisional recognition and in 1971 championship status was granted by the CCF. There followed a few years of show success and the first Sphynx champion was Dutchie's Nefertiti. The breed was always controversial; kittens were difficult to rear and the most viable ones were male. Eventually CFA revoked the provisional recognition and the Sphynx remained a minority breed – in fact it was widely believed that the strain had died out in the USA.

However a breeder named Hernandez had moved to the Netherlands and taken six cats of Sphynx pedigree with him. At least one of these went to Tonia Vink of Rotterdam and another was acquired by the French breeder, Patrick Challain. A breeding programme commenced in France and continued in Holland.

When in 1984 Vicki and Peter Markstein of the Petmark cattery in New York visited Guy Pantigny and Patrick Challain they saw the Sphynx family and, in their words 'it was love at first sight'. When the Marksteins returned home a Sphynx went with them, was given the name E.T. for publicity purposes and became an instant celebrity. Large numbers of New Yorkers visited the 1985 TICA show at the Maidson Square Garden to see him.

Recently an eight-year-old Dutch female was sold to a British breeder by Tonia Vink and plans have been made to establish the breed in the GCCF.

In every case breeders have experienced problems in rearing kittens and thus the Sphynx still remains a rare breed, adored by those who are fascinated by its quaintness but abhored by others who consider it to be a freak and worry about the problems presented in its breeding.

Folklore

The Jesuit Fathers of New Mexico claimed in 1902 that there was a hairless Aztec breed of cats known only in New Mexico and that the cats owned by F. J. Shinick were the last survivors of this ancient breed.

Conformation

Of slender build with a wedge-shaped head, short muzzle and a skull flat between the eyes. Kittens have wrinkles on the head and on the loose skin of the body. In adult cats the skin feels like suede to the touch and is wrinkled only on the head, neck and legs. Judges require adult cats to be virtually free of wrinkles on the body.

Coat

Although the breed is described as hairless this is not completely true. The adult cat has fur on the back of the ears, on the tip of the tail and on the paws up to the ankles. Absence of hair in these parts is considered a fault.

Colours

All colours are bred but the white areas of the normal cat are shown by pink areas of skin and black areas show as grey. Other skin colours relate to other coat colours.

Patterns

All patterns are bred and although the body is hairless the skin is patterned according to the basic coat pattern.

Eyes

Green, yellow, golden or copper, in accordance with skin/coat colour.

Personality

Described in the TICA 86 Show programme as the most loving cat it is possible to meet.

Voice

Usually moderate but decidedly vocal on occasion.

Kittens

Born with loose wrinkled skin covered with soft, fine hair which almost completely disappears as they become adult. By the time the cat is fully grown the body has become hard, muscular and smooth.

Show Status

Accepted as a provisional breed by CFA but this was subsequently revoked. Recognized by CCFA in 1971 and by the CCA. Accepted for registration as a new breed and colour by TICA in 1985 which is now the only USA body to do so. Recognized for championships by some independent clubs of Europe. Not recognized in Britain although the GCCF has accepted the breed for registration. Not accepted by the CA of Britain or by the FIFe.

Breeding

British breeders in GCCF breed only to Devon and Cornish Rex. Breeding programmes elsewhere vary.

Black and white bi-colour Sphynx

Tonkinese

Name
The name was taken from the Gulf of Tonkin in the South China Sea on the opposite coast to those of Burma and Siam (Thailand) in the Bay of Bengal in order to evoke the Burmese and Siamese but at the same time to demonstrate that while the Tonkinese has some of their qualities it is a breed in its own right. In the early days of the breed it was also known as Golden Siamese.

Origins
Early breeding records of the Burmese programme demonstrate the fact that the founder cat of the Burmese breed was actually a Tonkinese and that many of the cats registered as Burmese in the early years of that breed were also Tonkinese. In fact championship status for the Burmese was revoked for a time in the late 1940s (in CFA) for that very reason. Subsequently Milan Greer, the author of *Fabulous Felines*, bred and exhibited Tonkinese under the name Golden Siamese, and wrote that his studies extended for five generations from the hybrid cross of Siamese and Burmese. Some time later two American breeders, Mrs Edith Lux and Mrs Robert Nelson, started work on a similar breeding programme and Mrs Lux proposed the breed name Tonkinese. They found it was possible to breed the Tonkinese shape quite consistently but that the Tonkinese colouring cannot breed because it results from a formula which combines the two genes for Burmese and Siamese colouring in a special way. While some kittens in litter have two genes for Burmese colouring, others have two genes for Siamese colouring and only a few have one gene for each. The breeding policy thus adopted by all associations recognizing the breed was that after an initial cross between Siamese and Burmese to produce 100 per cent Tonkinese, further matings should be only Tonkinese to Tonkinese in order to achieve the ratio in litters of fifty per cent Tonkinese and fifty per cent Tonkinese variant. The variants assort into fifty per cent Siamese pointed and fifty per cent Burmese coated. In 1965 Margaret Conroy of Ontario, Canada, started work with Tonkinese and largely as a result of her efforts the CCA was the first to accept the breed for championship competition.

Conformation
Medium-sized. Well-muscled with slender legs and a long tapering tail, wider at the base than at the tip. The head has a modified wedge with a squarish muzzle and a slight nose break when seen from the side. The ears are rounded at the tips, pricked forward and of medium size. The eyes are almond-shaped and slightly Oriental.

Coat
Short, close-lying and silky to the touch.

Colours
In Canada and the USA: natural mink; champagne; mink; blue mink; platinum mink; honey mink. In Britain: seal; blue; chocolate; lilac; red; cream; tortie.

Eyes
Aquamarine.

Variation
Coats darken with age but change very little as a result of seasonal variation in temperature or humidity. Cats of the paler colours may not develop their true colouring until they reach sixteen months to two years of age.

Personality
The clown of the cat fancy.

Voice
Rather strident.

Kittens
Kittens are born much lighter than they will become as adults, the actual colouring varying with the basic colour alleles. Eyes are blue in babyhood and develop to aquamarine. Blue eyes or yellow eyes in adolescence denote that the cat is a Tonkinese variant rather than a Tonkinese.

Show Status
First recognized by the CCA. Recognized in the USA by the CFF in 1975. Accepted as championship breed by the ICA in 1979. Accepted for registration with CFA in 1978 and now a championship CFA breed. Accepted as a provisional breed, without championship status, by the CA of Britain in 1986.

Breeding
Only Tonkinese and Tonkinese variants are allowed in Tonkinese pedigrees for championship competition. Siamese, Burmese, Tonkinese variants and Tonkinese are allowed in pedigrees in Britain while the breed is without championship status. Tonkinese-bred kittens with points and blue eyes or with Burmese coats and yellow eyes are Tonkinese variants and are not eligible for Tonkinese classes.

Natural mink (seal) Tonkinese

The Oriental Group

The Oriental group includes all the varieties developed from cats originating in Siam (now Thailand). In some colour is mostly restricted to the points – the Siamese – and in others colour and pattern are dispersed all over the body – the Oriental Shorthair.

It is well documented that cats have always been admired by the people of the Orient. Manuscripts on display in the National Library of Bangkok illustrate the diversity of colours and patterns among the cats of the medieval Siamese capital, Ayudhya. They show that the Siamese cats were of much lighter build than those of Europe and that, although most of the colour varieties known in Europe were present, there were also cats with colour restricted to face, ears, legs and tail which were considered by the Siamese to be sufficiently special to be selected to live in the royal palaces.

Many of the cats first exported from Siam are reputed to have been gifts from the King. Owners of Foreign Whites like to believe that their variety was also under royal protection, quoting the writer M. Oldfield Howery who wrote in his book *Mysteries of Religion and Magic*: 'Ancestor worship is still an impelling force in Oriental countries. It was probably in order to show reverence to the departed monarch that when the young King of Siam was crowned in 1926 a white cat was carried by the court chamberlains in the procession to the throne room. Even today the

Burmese and Siamese believe that the beautiful sacred cats enshrine the spirits of the dead, so, when a member of the royal house of Siam was buried, one of his favourite cats used to be entombed with him.'

In the Ayudhya manuscripts the pointed cat is illustrated and described as having a black tail, black feet and black ears with otherwise white hair and reddish eyes. But the pointed variety was not the only Siamese cat. In fact every variety of Oriental Shorthair was recorded in ancient Siam – even the bi-colours, known in Ayudhya as Singhasep, and the harlequins which were known by the Siamese as 'nine-points' because they had nine areas of colour on a basically white body.

Popular legends concerning the Siamese abound. It was said that the kink in its tail came about because the royal princesses, when bathing, used their cats' tails to hold their rings and the kinks developed to stop them falling off. Another legend explains: 'The sacred cats of the temple were left by a priest to guard a valuable temple vase. They guarded it with such zeal that the steadfast staring caused the cats' eyes to cross and their tails curled round the vase to become kinked.'

The first Siamese taken to Europe and the USA included both pointed and solid colour cats. Harrison Weir described two kinds of Siamese among the early imports: 'the dun Siamese with body of a dun colour, nose, part of the face, ears, feet and tail of a very dark chocolate brown, nearly black, eyes of a beautiful blue by day and red by night', and another kind 'of a very rich chocolate or seal with darker face, ears and tail; the legs are a shade darker which intensifies towards the feet. The eyes small, of a rich amber colour'. The cats from Siam arrived at the start of the cat fancy and the organization of the first cat shows and their unusual looks assured them of instant attention. At the National Cat Show of 1879 the British *Daily Telegraph* reported on 'a yet more curious, if less prepossessing, couple of juveniles of Siamese extraction with black muzzles, ears, feet and tail setting off a close, yellowish drab coat and completing the resemblance of the little brutes to a pair of pug puppies'.

The Siamese Cat Club was formed in Britain in 1901 and drew up the first standards for Siamese in 1902. Early pedigree registers record the fact that not all Siamese cats bred were pointed, but by the end of the 1920s the club ruled that only the blue-eyed cats could be called Siamese and the others, now known as the Orientals, were consigned to oblivion – or so the club officials thought. In Britain the only Siamese colour officially allowed at early shows was the seal point; but in 1936, the campaigners for the blue point won the day and championship status was granted.

The first Siamese champion was a seal point named Wankee. He was born in Hong Kong in 1895 and had a kinked tail. The first blue point to become a champion was Sayo of Bedale bred by Mrs Phil Wade. The chocolate point was belatedly recognized as a colour variety rather than a poor seal in 1950 and ten years later championship status was granted for the lilac pointed Siamese. Six years later the red point, tortie point and every colour of tabby point were recognized in Britain and more recently the cream point gained the right to high honours.

In the USA the history of the Siamese followed a similar pattern and the first breed standard and breed club were modelled on their British counterparts. Then in 1914 the Americans drew up their own standard and evolved their own pattern of shows and showing. Many well known British breeders sent stock to the USA and one such cat was the famous seal point champion, Oriental Nankie Pooh of Newton. He lived to be seventeen and was said to have sired over 1,300 kittens. When he died the Americans held a show in his honour. In the USA tabby points, red and cream points and tortie points are known in some associations as colourpoint shorthairs rather than as Siamese, and the tabby variety is described as the Lynx.

All over the world the pointed cats ruled the Siamese cat fancy until in the 1950s an enterprising breeder named Mrs Armitage Hargreaves mated Siamese to Russian Blue and bred the first Oriental blacks. Then when Mrs Monro-Smith mated a seal point to a domestic longhair and bred an Oriental black named Elmtower Susannah, plans were made for the reincarnation of the foreign type chocolate brown and the breeding programme later to produce the Havana of the USA and the Oriental chocolate variety was under way. The blacks were ignored at that time other than as breeding stock but the chocolate browns attained championship recognition in 1958 under the name Chestnut Brown Foreign.

In Britain Patricia Turner of the Scintilla cattery commenced a breeding programme towards a blue-eyed white Siamese-type white shorthair, and was soon joined by Jane Flack of the Monach cattery in Northern Ireland and Phyllis Dawson of the Elmham cattery in Norfolk. The three breeders developed separate breeding lines in order that the foundation cats should not be too inbred and a new line evolved when Ann Codrington of the Watermill cattery mated a white British Shorthair to Siamese. In due course the new breed was admitted to championship circles under the name of Foreign White. Until the Seychellois was bred the Foreign White was the only blue-eyed Siamese-type cat not to have Siamese points.

Once there were Orientals in chocolate brown and white it was only a matter of time before other colour varieties evolved. A new line of Oriental-type havanas and lilacs was developed, largely as a result of work by Angela Sayer of the Solitaire cattery, and in 1970 the Chestnut Brown was formally re-named as Havana. The change delighted those who had always preferred the original name for the breed but caused great difficulties for internationally-minded cat fanciers who also knew of the non-Oriental type Havana in the USA.

Matings between Oriental Shorthairs with chocolate brown coats and tabby point Siamese led to Oriental tabbies, Oriental blacks and Oriental blues. In 1970 an accidental mating between a Siamese and a Silver Chinchilla Persian led to Patricia Turner starting another breeding project, this time for the silver shaded, silver tabby and smoke varieties of Oriental, and leading eventually to the breeding of golden Orientals and the development of a completely new colour named caramel. Cats of this programme were exported to all parts of the world and have given rise to the caramel, smoke, silver tabby and shaded silver varieties of Siamese which are already recognized in some associations.

In most associations all varieties of Oriental Shorthair have the same breed name, but the GCCF in Britain decided that in their association the name Oriental would be reserved for cats with patterned coats and the name Foreign would be used for the rest. Thus in GCCF there are Siamese, Oriental Shorthairs and Foreign Shorthairs, all with Oriental body type.

The most recent Oriental variety is the Seychellois (see page 108). It developed from a breeding programme started in 1984 by Patricia Turner, for blue-eyed Oriental-type white cats with dashes and splashes of colour on their bodies and coloured tails. They are bred in shorthair and in semi-longhair. Their colour patterns are known genetically as the 'Seychelles patterns' – hence the variety's name. During the Seychellois breeding programme Oriental bi-colours, tortie and whites and harlequins were bred in Britain; and both there and in the Netherlands, France and the USA a number of breeders work specifically on this variety.

American breeders have recently become interested in re-creating the wide range of varieties that originally populated Siam. Oriental Shorthairs were imported from Britain and new crosses made between Siamese and American Shorthair. The Americans put such dedication and enthusiasm into the project that they gained championship recognition in a large number of colours very quickly. A group of breeders is now campaining for recognition for the original type of Siamese alongside the present-day types; but because they are so different the traditional Siamese must for the time being be exhibited at shows in the section for 'New Breed and Colour'!

Although some associations recognize more than others the basic list of varieties is –

Siamese

Seal, blue, chocolate, cinnamon, lilac, fawn, caramel, the tortie varieties of all those colours, red and cream.

Seal tabby, blue tabby, chocolate tabby, cinnamon tabby, lilac tabby, fawn tabby, caramel tabby, the torbie varieties of all those colours, red tabby and cream tabby.

Seal silver tabby, blue silver tabby, chocolate silver tabby, cinnamon silver tabby, lilac silver tabby, fawn silver tabby, caramel silver tabby, the torbie varieties of all these colours, red silver tabby and cream silver tabby.

Oriental Shorthair

Black, blue, chocolate (Havana), cinnamon, lilac, fawn, caramel, the tortie varieties of these colours, red and cream.

Black tabby (known in GCCF as brown tabby), blue tabby, chocolate tabby, cinnamon tabby, lilac tabby, fawn tabby, caramel tabby, the tortie varieties of these colours, red and cream.

Tabbies are bred in four patterns – ticked, mackerel, spotted and classic (blotched).

Shaded and tipped silvers in all basic colours; shaded and tipped goldens in all basic colours; smokes in all basic colours; bi-colours and harlequins in all basic colours with white; blue-eyed Whites (Foreign White); Seychellois shorthair.

Cinnamon Oriental Shorthair

Name
The breed name was chosen by British breeders to denote cats of Siamese conformation but lacking Siamese points pattern. The colour name of Cinnamon denotes the similarity of the coat colour to the spice. Also known as Foreign Cinnamon in one or two cat fancy organizations. Formerly known as Caramels in the USA and blonde Havanas in the Netherlands.

Origins
The Cinnamon Oriental Shorthair owes its existence to Dutch and British breeders who set out to research the genetics of the reddish brown colour known then as red in the Abyssinian breed (see page 54). In the Netherlands in the 1960s Maria Falkena of the Mariendaal cattery test mated her red Abyssinian queen and an Havana of the British breeding programme. The kittens were ticked tabby, one chocolate and the other two black. From matings with these kittens Maria Falkena and others including Mevr Wielenga and the Boekhorsts bred generations of cats, some cinnamon and some of other colours.

Most Dutch breeders disapproved of the cinnamons and so the kittens were neutered and sold as family pets. But, in 1979 Maria Falkena heard of a litter bred by Stibbe-Lienman which included two cinnamon males. After researching the pedigree to find the source of the cinnamon colour she realized that it had been inherited from her own breeding programme and contacted her to offer her a male kitten. As a result the cinnamon gradually evolved as an Oriental variety.

Although the British programme started later than that in the Netherlands the motivation was identical – to solve the puzzle of two red colours in cats. Maureen and Roy Silson, Siamese breeders who owned the Southview cattery, acquired two cross-bred Abyssinian/Siamese cats and mated them together. The result was the first cinnamon in Britain. Later one of the two cross breds was mated to an albino Siamese imported from the USA to found a long line of Southview Orientals with chocolate coat colour but who were carrying the cinnamon gene. For a while the British cat fancy programme was also slowed, nearly to a stop, by prejudice. It was not the cinnamon colour that was disliked but rather the albino Siamese, known by that time as recessive white. The GCCF applied various types of sanction against breeding stock with albino Siamese background. However, just as in Holland, the cinnamon colour re-appeared in litters from chocolate cats and this time a preservation and development programme was organized. New enthusiasts joined the project and success was assured.

The colour is now bred worldwide, although its name was only recently agreed. It was at a meeting of the GCCF Genetics Committee, when

Patricia Turner produced colour photographs of cinnamon cats, a bar of milk chocolate, a bar of plain chocolate and a pot of cinnamon sticks, that the committee agreed on cinnamon. Later it emerged that in the Netherlands the name had been inspired by the colour of cinnamon biscuits.

Conformation
Svelte and lithe with elegant lines to a slender body, thin whippy tail and long, slim legs. The head is long with a wedge-shaped muzzle and the ears are large and set wide on the head.

Coat
Very short, silky and close lying.

Colours
Cinnamon.

Eyes
Bright green.

Personality
Bright, intelligent and very demanding.

Voice
Sometimes well modulated, other times raucous.

Kittens
Born with cinnamon coats although the shine that develops on the coat of the adult is not apparent in the tiny kitten. When eyes first open their colour is blue. This gradually changes through grey to greyish green to green. Yellow eyes are considered a fault.

Show Status
First granted championship status by the NKFV of the Netherlands in 1980. Now a championship breed in all other independent clubs of Europe, the USA and in the CA of Britain. Recognized for championship in the member countries of FIFe but not in the GCCF of Britain.

Breeding
Oriental Shorthairs of all colours and Siamese of all colours are allowed in pedigrees. A number of registration bodies also allow Javanese (longhair Orientals) and Balinese (longhair Siamese).

Blue Point Siamese

Name
Named after the original name for Thailand, where the cat fancy Siamese originated. Blue has been used since time immemorial to describe a bluish grey coat colour in animals.

Origins
Blue grey coat colour was recorded by artists in Thailand in the fourteenth century and one of the first cat fanciers to define it was Harrison Weir who wrote 'blue in cats is one of the most extraordinary colours of any, for it is a mixture of black, which is no colour, and white, which is no colour . . .' Britain's national blue point register opened on 21 June 1894 with a Siamese named Rhoda. In these early years of the breed there were casualties from infection and many cats and kittens died soon after they returned from shows. During the First World War British stock dwindled to become almost non-existent but by that time Siamese had become established in the USA and after the 1918 armistice US breeders sent stock to Britain to help in the re-building of the breed.

Because the blue colour is inherited in a recessive manner, the birth of a blue point from seal point parents was often unexpected and the variety came to be known as 'sports' or 'freaks'. As early as 1896 Louis Wain had refused to judge a Siamese on grounds that it was blue and when the first book on Siamese was written by Phil Wade she wrote, 'Even the best blue pointed cannot, I think, equal the beauty of our seal pointed cats and I can see no real object in trying to breed them. Their value at the moment is their scarcity but I cannot believe there will ever be a great demand for them.' But not all Siamese breeders agreed with her and by the early 1930s numbers were increasing. Mrs Cox-Ife, a famous breeder of the time, championed them and advertised the services of two blue pointed studs.

In 1934 *Fur and Feather* magazine stated: 'Not a great deal is known about blue pointed Siamese, and the more breeders express their views the quicker we shall arrive at full knowledge of the influence of these charming creatures. . . .' The request was heeded, and nearly thirty years after the first blue points were recorded the GCCF recognized the blue point variety of Siamese for championship on 19 February 1936. The first blue pointed champion was Sayo of Bedale, bred by Mrs Wade and owned by Mrs Greta Hindley.

In 1944 Greta Hindley founded the Blue Pointed Siamese Cat Club. Among the founder members were Major and Mrs Rendall of the Misselfore cattery, whose cats became ancestors of show winners for countless British breeders in later decades.

Siamese are first recorded in the USA when one was purchased by Mrs Rutherford B. Hayes. A Mrs Blanche Arral of New Jersey is said to have been presented with a pair of Siamese by the King of Siam, but two of the earliest of the breed to be formerly recorded were Lockhaven Siam and Lockhaven Sally Ward owned by Mrs Clinton Locke of Chicago. Just as in Britain blue points were often regarded as 'sports'. Only after a revised breed standard was drawn up by Virginia Cobb and the National Siamese Cat Club was the blue variety understood and accepted. By 1932 separate Blue Point Siamese classes were offered at shows of the CFA.

Conformation
Elegant, lithe and yet muscular with a long slender body set on tall slim legs with spoon-shaped paws. The tail is long, thin and tapering. The head is longer than in other breeds (except the Oriental Shorthair) and, in European Siamese the head forms a triangle in space with the apex being at the chin when seen from the front. In Siamese of North America the Siamese head generally has a longer muzzle and the ears are set higher. The body is more tubular, the legs are even more slender and the tail is even longer.

Coat
Very short and silky, lying close to the body.

Colours and Patterns
Light bluish grey mask, ears, legs and tail known as 'the points' with a greyish cream body colour which shades imperceptibly into the blue.

Eyes
Vivid blue.

Personality
Unforgettably domineering, affectionate and demanding of human attention at all times.

Voice
Very vocal and with a strong 'miaoooow'.

Kittens
Born nearly white and the grey blue colour is first seen on the tail and ear tips as the kitten develops. The colour gets deeper and the degree of colour extends throughout kittenhood so that in the adolescent the full Siamese coat pattern is seen. Voice alters from kitten squeaks to the full, rich tones of the adult.

Show Status
Recognized as a championship variety of the Siamese in Britain in 1936. Now recognized world wide.

Breeding
In the CFA three generation pedigrees must include only Siamese of the colours seal, blue, chocolate or lilac. Elsewhere three generation pedigrees may include Siamese or Oriental Shorthair although some organizations penalise Siamese with Orientals in their pedigree by entering them on to a supplementary register. Some organizations also allow Siamese pedigrees to include Javanese (longhair Orientals) and Balinese (longhair Siamese). ·

The Semi-Longhair Group

The Semi-Longhair group includes all those longhair cats with coats slightly shorter and often without the definite undercoat of the Persian. Some, like the Balinese and Javanese, have extreme Oriental type, some, like the Norwegian Forest Cat, have moderate type and others, like the Siberian, have type very similar to the Persians of the nineteenth century.

Some have been protectively bred to retain as many as possible of their natural characteristics. These are the Birman, the Maine Coon, the Norwegian Forest Cat, the Russian Angora, the Siberian, the Turkish Angora and the Turkish Van. Others represent the longhaired mutants of earlier shorthair breeds; these are the Balinese (the longhaired variety of Siamese); Cymric (the longhaired variety of Manx), Scottish Fold Longhair; Somali (the longhaired variety of Abyssinian). A longhaired Burmese variety, known by American breeders as Tiffany, is actually a colour of Asian Longhair (see page 92); and three potential new group members are the Nebelung, a longhaired variety of Russian type, the provisionally named Suqutranese, which can best be described as a White Somali, and the American Bobtail.

prepared the Angoras from Turkey were very much in evidence, although they were later inter-bred with heavier type longhairs and lost their identity as a pedigree breed. In 1962, after imports were made direct to the USA from the Ankara Zoo by Thomas and Virginia Torio, American breeders began to appreciate their beauty again and after additional imports sufficient foundation stock was bred to evolve the now well-known Turkish Angora. In the USSR, the home of the original longhair domesticated cats, Angoras are well known, although their history is not fully documented. Nikolai Nepomnyashchi of the Fauna Cat Lovers Association in Moscow has reported that the main difference between the Turkish Angora and the Russian Angora is that the latter often have green eyes.

White Turkish Angoras are sometimes deaf, especially if they have blue eyes, the fact that the breed survived for so many centuries suggests that deafness is more of a handicap than a serious defect. Although in an ideal world all white cats would have full hearing the only way to accomplish this would be to breed in another type of blue eye by outcrosses to the Siamese patterned breed; but this would go against all the breeding policies for the Turkish Angora.

Others in the group are the American Curl, a near-domestic form in which curly ears mutated; and the several breeds contrived by careful re-combination of existing colour, pattern and coat length characteristics, such as the Ragdoll, Seychellois longhair and the rare Tibetan which is a Birman-type breed without Birman pattern.

Although all members of the group have long hair there is great variation in this characteristic with some breeds having appreciably longer coats at all times of the year and others appearing nearly shorthaired, other than on the tail during the hotter months. Coat texture also varies between breeds, as does the degree of undercoat. As a result grooming techniques also vary.

The oldest breeds in the group are probably the Birman, Cymric, Maine Coon, Norwegian Forest Cat, Siberian and the Russian and Turkish Angora. The Turkish Van is in fact a colour variety of Turkish Angora which has evolved to have somewhat different breed type, and it is likely that both the Maine Coon and the Norwegian Forest Cat have their origin in the Siberian, the native breed of the USSR where the longhair gene first mutated. However the age of the breed bears little relation to its period of seniority in the cat fancy, so that some of the oldest breeds have been only recently recognized and the oldest two are still regarded as 'unrecognized'.

When the first cat shows were held and standards for judging were

In an illustration from Buffon's *Histoire Naturelle*, published in 1756, a tabby Angora is shown with head length, body size and shape very similar to the Turkish Angora except that the ears were set decidedly lower than in the present day show cat. The original colours of the Turkish Angora were red tabby, black tabby (brown tabby), silver tabby, black, red, tortie, tortie and white and white. In Turkish Angoras, Russian Angoras and Turkish Van the hairs of both topcoat and undercoat are very soft and there is no woolliness in the latter. Coat length may reach 15cm on some parts of the body and, although there are ruff, breeches and a full tail the fall of the coat follows the lines of the body because of this lack of woolly padding. The tail is referred to as a plume rather than as a brush for the same reason.

The Maine Coon, originally known as the Maine cat, was very much to the fore of the early cat fancy. The colours bred were similar to those of domestic cats of Britain and Europe, from which the breed originated. Maine cats had their own shows long before the US cat fancy officially started. The coat of the Maine Coon is thick and glossy and has very little undercoat. The top coat is rather coarse and tends to increase in length towards the tail which is plumed. Although there is a frontal ruff beginning at the base of the ears the Coon is not expected to own a full ruff as seen in Persians. Grooming techniques vary between the colour varieties but care is always taken to avoid imparting an apparently Persian coat texture by over-softening the hairs of the top coat. Although in early years the Coons were described as shaggy (they even had an alternative name Shag), judges now expect to see every hair falling separately. Because of its lack of woolly undercoat knots in a Coon coat are not usually a problem.

Another ancient breed is the Birman, also known as the Sacred Cat of Burma. Breed historians recount that the first Birmans were taken to France by Major Gordon Russell in 1911 but recognition as a breed was not granted until after the Second World War (see page 96). They are difficult to breed to the standard which requires a white pattern seen as gloves tipping the toes and also extending up the back of the legs towards a point near the hock joint on the rear legs. The breed has the typical head width of the original Russian longhairs but has a characteristic profile quite different from that of any other breed. Although the Birman is blue eyed the brilliance and depth of colour found in the Siamese is rarely achieved, many cats having eyes of a rather greyish blue.

Virtually identical in breed type to the Birman is the Tibetan, which was first bred as a result of outcrosses to Persian during breeding programmes for new colours. A few breeders decided to promote the new variety by backcrossing to Birman to improve Birman type but selecting against Birman-marked kittens for breeding stock. Although provisional recognition was granted by the CA of Britain in 1986 very few examples of Tibetan have been shown in recent years.

The Cymric (see page 98) is the longhaired form of Manx and shares the Manx dense padded undercoat and harsh, glossy top coat. It is best known in the USA where it is championed by Vicki Hansen, whose Cathro Cym White Boy of Pussnbooze became one of the top twenty cats in TICA. A similar coat is found in the Norwegian Forest Cat. Norwegians are classified in four classes at shows – one for cats with agouti (tabby) coats; another for cats with smoke, tortie or solidly coloured coats; a third for cats with agouti and white coats and the fourth for cats with smoke and white, tortie and white or solidly coloured and white coats. Historians suggest that the breed descended from Scottish wildcats brought to Norway by the Vikings, but it may simply have evolved from the Siberian of neighbouring Russia.

The Balinese was developed from Siamese lines carrying the recessive longhair gene. Many of its ancestors were Siamese from Britain where it is recorded in the history of the Havana (see page 66) that Mrs Monro-Smith of the Elmtower cattery made matings with longhaired domestics and Siamese. Not so generally known is that some of the progeny were later used for breeding Siamese. Today many winning lines of Siamese trace their ancestry to Elmtower Bronze Idol, a stud of the early Havana breeding programme. The coat of the Balinese is considerably shorter than in other semi-longhairs and it has only a rudimentary undercoat. It is therefore very easy to groom – most of the work being undertaken by the cat.

Some US associations refer to the tabby, tortie and red varieties of Balinese as Javanese; but this breed name is widely used by other associations to describe the Oriental Longhair. The Seychellois (see page 108) currently being developed under the direction of Patricia Turner in Britain is a colour and white variety of Oriental with either long or short hair.

The Somali was developed largely at the instigation of Evelyn Mague of New Jersey in the USA and was first recognized for championships there in 1979. Soon after that it was afforded breed status internationally by the FIFe and in Britain by the CA. It still remains rare, not recognized for championship competition by the GCCF. A cat of Abyssinian type, it has a long silky textured coat with each hair banded and ticked up to twelve times. The ruddy colour is genetically black tabby, but selective breeding by Abyssinian breeders over the past hundred years has evolved the warm rufous tone to the coat. Eastern European breeders recommend the addition of paprika to the diet in order to promote the development of ticking in the coat. If paprika is given care should be taken to use the sweet Hungarian variety rather than the hot pepper sold in many stores.

The Ragdoll stands on its own in the Semi-longhair group as a breed with a distinctive and individual breed type and with three different coat patterns (see page 106). Although developed from crosses made by Ann Baker between two other breeds, it has emerged as entirely different from both of them. Its magnificent coat, when in prime condition, is hard to beat and in Britain it has the reputation of being the best 'turned out' breed of the group. At present it is not fully recognized outside the USA and the CA in Britain; but there is also an active group of breeders in Germany and recognition by FIFe should be a possibility within the next few years.

The Scottish Fold longhair first occurred in Scotland in the early 1960s and later journeyed to the USA where it has become a very popular breed. Once numbers in the breed were high members of the TICA began showing them in New Breed and Colour classes. In 1986 the Scottish Fold Breed Section in TICA voted 39–1 to accept the Longhair Scottish Fold for championship competition and this became effective from May 1987.

The American Curl was first bred in longhair (see American Curl Shorthair on page 22) and is now recognized in the USA and some independent associations of Europe in both coat lengths. The Nebelung is not recognized in any association but is now advertised for sale in the USA. The Suqutranese made its debut at a show of the CA of Britain on 17 March 1990, when Mrs C. Garrard of the Chiwanda cattery and Charles and Betty Barrett of the Betic cattery exhibited cats of Chiwanda breeding. The Suqutranese has the conformation, coat length and texture of the Somali but the Somali ticked coat is replaced by one of dazzling white.

The grooming of the semi-longhairs varies slightly between colours and breeds but in all breeds the aim is for each hair to glisten with good health and for the coat to be totally free of scurf, dust or excess oil. Bathing with mild coconut oil shampoo, followed by the use of an appropriate conditioner, and drying with the help of a moisture absorbing cloth helps to get the coat dry without making it too fluffy.

Asian Longhair

Name
Named by British breeders to denote the Burmese-type longhair. Asian Longhairs with the Burmese coat pattern are also known as Tiffany or Longhair Burmese

Origins
Very little is known about the origins of the Tiffany. It is known to be a longhair variety with Burmese conformation and coat colouring but the means by which the long hair was achieved in the original cats of the USA is not clear. Tiffanies were advertised in US cat fancy managazines in the mid 1970s as 'long haired Burmese' and a photograph of two of them was featured in the 1979 *Book of the Cat*. Since that date little has been heard of the American lines but the British breeding programme for Asian Shorthairs (see Burmilla, page 00) brought together genes for long hair and Burmese coat colour so that when type became refined towards the true Burmese the occurrence of Asian Longhairs and Tiffanies was inevitable. The first breeder to obtain Tiffany in that programme was Jeanne Bryson of the Favagello cattery in Droitwich, Worcester, while non-Burmese coloured Asian Longhairs were bred by a number of breeders including Therese and Charles Clarke of the Kartush cattery in Oxfordshire and Marion and Alan Lomas of the Newtimber cattery in Sussex.

However the Clarkes and the Lomases were following a breeding programme designed specifically for the production of Burmillas so that when kittens with coats that were not shorthaired shaded or tipped silver were born they were sold as pets and neutered. A shaded silver Asian Longhair won high honours in CA pet classes for Marion and Alan Lomas and Kartush Abeche, a blue Asian Longhair bred by the Clarkes and owned by Mrs Southwell was to find fame when described in a popular book on cats as a sable brown Tiffany.

In 1986 the Asian Longhair (including Tiffany) was granted medallist status by the CA of Britain but since that date very few cats have been shown and the variety remains rare.

Conformation
Identical to the Burmese in every respect.

Coat
Long, fine and silky, longer and fuller on the ruff, breeches and tail.

Colours
Brown (sable); blue, chocolate, lilac, red, cream, all tortie versions of these colours; all colours of silver in tabby, shaded and tipped; all colours of golden in tabby, shaded and tipped; all colours of smoke.

Patterns
Solid colours; Burmese shaded; tabbies in ticked, mackerel, spotted and classic (blotched); torties; torbies; shadeds; tippeds; smoke.

Eyes
Green in all Asian Longhairs other than Tiffany. Any shade of yellow from chartreuse to amber, with golden yellow preferred in Tiffanies.

Variation
Body conformation varies between the heavier type of the USA where the heavier American style Burmese is bred and the lighter boned type of Britain and Europe where the European style Burmese is bred.

Kittens
All kittens are born with short coats and the length develops gradually over the first few months. Tiffany kittens are born with coats much lighter than in the adult so that brown kittens are born café-au-lait.

Personality
Bombastic, athletic and bossy.

Voice
Moderate in general conversation but quite strident when hungry or thwarted.

Show Status
All Asian Longhairs, including the Tiffany, may compete at shows in member countries of the FIFe where they can also compete for the show title 'Best unrecognized breed'. They are eligible for medallist titles in the CA of Britain. The Tiffany may compete in the USA in 'New Breed and Colour Classes'. Also shown as a new breed in some independent clubs in Europe. Not recognised by the GCCF.

Breeding
Only Tiffany and Burmese in USA Tiffany pedigrees. Only Burmese and Asian (either longhair or shorthair) in Asian Longhair pedigrees in the CA of Britain and in some of the independent clubs of Europe. The GCCF has not yet published a breeding policy.

Sorrel silver Asian Longhair

Balinese

Name
Named after the graceful dancers of Bali. Formerly known as Longhaired Siamese. Some colours known as Javanese in the USA.

Origins
The first Balinese kittens were the unexpected longhaired result of matings between Siamese and the first breeder recorded is Marion Dorsey of the Rai Mar cattery in California. She is said to have bred longhaired Siamese as early as the 1940s. Records confirm that she was definitely breeding them by 1955. Some six years later Helen Smith of the Merry Mews cattery in New York exhibited a Longhaired Siamese at the Empire Cat Show and shortly after that the two breeders began a collaboration. The breed name Longhaired Siamese proved unpopular with the breeders of Siamese, and as Bali is geographically near to Thailand (originally Siam) and the graceful plume-tailed cats evoked memories of the dancers of Bali the breed name Balinese proposed by Helen Smith was accepted. Shortly after this Helen Smith sold up to Sylvia Holland of the Holland's Farm cattery, also in California, who became an ardent supporter of the Balinese cause. Other pioneer breeders were Mildred Davis of the Cedar Cliffe cattery, Ruby Breen of the Verde cattery, Elcy Crouch of the E.L.C. Kats cattery and Elaine Young of the Ti-Mau cattery. In 1968 the club known as The Balinese Breeders and Fans International was formed, more fanciers joined the ranks of those actively breeding and exhibiting the little Balis and the future of the breed was assured.

News of the beautiful Balinese spread to Europe and in the mid-1970s cats were sent to Britain to form the basis of a breeding programme which involved matings to Siamese to improve type and widen the gene pool. Similarly Balinese emigrated to the Netherlands and other European countries.

Conformation
Slender and elegant with a long body set on long slim legs. The head is long, with a wedged muzzle and large ears set so that their outer edges are in line with the outer lines of the head and muzzle to form a triangular shape.

Coat
Medium-long, fine and silky, lying close to the body and with longer coat at the breeches and on the tail, which is plumed.

Colours
Seal point; blue point; chocolate point; lilac point; the tortie; tabby and torbie versions of these colours; red point; cream point. Some associations recognize additional colours while others recognize only seal, blue, chocolate or lilac. In the CFA of the USA the tabby, tortie, red and cream varieties are known as Javanese.

Patterns
Mask, stockings and tail of the basic colour with the body paler and shaded with tones of the basic colour. The darker coloured areas are known as 'the points'. This is the pattern known as Siamese or Himalayan. Points may be of solid colour or patterned in tortoiseshell, tabby or a combination of both (torbie).

Eyes
Bright blue.

Personality
Extrovert, very lively and a kitten throughout life, even into old age.

Voice
Never stops talking in a conversational miaow. Sometimes rather noisy when hungry or in season.

Kittens
Like other semi-longhaired breeds kittens are born with short hair which begins to become fluffy after the first two weeks. As in Siamese the newborn kittens are near white and the colour develops gradually over the first few weeks of life.

Show Status
First exhibited in the USA in 1961. Championship in all US associations achieved by 1970 and granted for the countries of FIFe and the CA of Britain in 1983. Championship status granted by the GCCF in 1984.

Breeding
Siamese, Balinese, Javanese and Oriental Shorthairs are allowed in Balinese pedigrees in most associations although in one or two associations only Balinese and Siamese are allowed.

Red point Balinese – flame point Javanese

Birman

Name
Birman (English); Sacré de Birmanie (French); Heilige Birmaan (Dutch). Also known as the Sacred Cat of Burma.

Origins
The Birman is said to have originated in western Burma; and certainly cats with similar markings are recorded in documents from ancient Thailand. One story claims that a pair was given as a gift to an Englishman named Major Gordon Russell and his friend August Pavie by the priests of the Khmer people; another that the cats were acquired by an American named Vanderbilt from a servant who had once been at the temple of Lao-Tsun where the cats were kept as sacred animals. Whatever the name of their new owners, most historians agree that the original two cats were shipped to France and that the male died on the way. The female, named Sita, is said to have been in kitten and to have produced a kitten named Poupée.

In 1925 it is recorded beyond doubt that the Fédération Féline Français recognized the Sacré de Birmanie as a championship breed. A photograph taken in 1930 shows a male of the day named Dieu d'Araken which became the blue-print for the breed. He was owned by M. Baudoin-Crevoisier, well known as a breeder of Birmans at that time. Later Dieu d'Araken was sold, together with six other Birmans, to Princess Ratibor and she subsequently left them in her will to the Duke d'Aosta. Eventually their ownership was transferred to the Countess Giriode Panissera and their pedigree line became famous worldwide. During the war M. Baudoin-Crevoisier managed to keep a few cats entire. His champion male Orlaff de Kaabaa and his female Xenia de Kaabaa became the breed's foundation cats.

In Germany a line of Birmans was maintained by Hanna Kreuger of the von Frohnau cattery and Liselotte von Warner of the von Irak cattery. Together with descendants of Orloff and Xenia they formed the nucleus of the post-war breeding stock.

The Birman first travelled to the USA in 1959 when Dr and Mrs Siepel of the Janacques cattery imported a male, Irrouaddi du Clos Fleuri.

Birmans arrived in Britain in 1964 when a male and two females were sent from France to Elsie Fisher and Margaret Richards. These two breeders registered a joint cattery name, Paranjoti.

Folklore
There are several versions of the Birman legend but the most widely repeated is that in the days before the coming of Buddha there lived at the temple of Lao-Tsun, in Indo-China, an old monk called Mun Ha who owned an orange-eyed white cat called Sinh and devoted his life to the sapphire-eyed goddess of migrating souls – Tsun-Kyan-Kse. When the temple was attacked by raiders Mun Ha and the other monks are said to have taken sanctuary in Tsun-Kyan-Kse, where Mun Ha died of shock. As he was dying the cat Sinh leapt upon his white head and a miracle occurred: the old man's soul entered the cat. The goddess granted the cat her own golden colour and sapphire blue eyes. Only where the cat's paws remained on the old monk's white head did its fur remain white.

Conformation
A medium-size cat, rather solidly built and with heavy legs and large round paws. The tail is carried high, often curved outwards like that of a squirrel. The shape of the head is considered to be of prime importance, with a broad, rounded skull and a forehead sloping back so that there is a flat spot in front of the ears. The face has full cheeks, a heavy jaw and a well-developed chin forming perpendicular lines with the upper lip. Seen from the side the nose is Roman, but there is a slight break in the profile at the level of the eyes.

Coat
The coat is semi-long, silky and without the woolly undercoat of the Persians. Ideally adult cats, especially males, should have a full ruff and a well-coated tail which is carried proudly like a plume.

Colours
Seal point; blue point; chocolate point; lilac point; red point; tortie point; tabby point.

Patterns
The unique Birman pattern combines the well-known Siamese mask, stockings and tail pattern with white gloves covering the toes on the front paws and white gauntlets covering the hind paws and extending up to the point of hock at the rear. One characteristic beloved of Birman breeders is a warm-toned suffusion of shading across the shoulders.

Eyes
As blue as possible.

Variation
Coat is much shorter in the hot weather but becomes fuller again during the winter months. Coats become more heavily shaded with age.

Personality
In general the Birman is a sweet-natured breed, loving to its owners, judges and other cats. However some breeding lines have resulted in cats which tend to be nervous and fearful and even aggressive when shown.

Kittens
Born nearly shorthaired and white or cream in colour. The colour points, the shading on the coat and the long hair develop as the kittens grow.

Show Status
Recognized and shown as a championship breed worldwide.

Breeding
Only Birmans are allowed in pedigrees.

Cymric

Name
Named in the USA after the Welsh name for Wales in order to suggest proximity to the Manx cat from the Isle of Man.

Origins
The breed shares its origin with the Manx, and the only difference between that breed and the Cymric is in coat length. Both longhaired and shorthaired kittens were, and are, bred on the Isle of Man. Only when longhaired kittens appeared in Manx litters bred in Canada was the breed name Cymric agreed and attempts made to gain show status for the variety, there and in the USA. One of the earliest campaigners was Althea Frahm of the Lovebunny cattery and her efforts were rewarded when Lovebunny Cymrics were listed in the All American Awards. One well-known winner of the 1970s was Champion Helle's Comus Jupiter, a copper-eyed white bred and owned by Blair Wright.

The zenith of the Cymric's career as an exhibition breed was a place in the Top Twenty cats of the ICA won by Vickie Hansen's Cathro Cym White Boy of Pussnbooze. White Boy was bred by Ron Cathro.

In Britain the Cymric has been quite successful in shows of the CA and a notable prizewinner in Medallist classes has been Elizabeth Price's own bred Polar Star, a white Cymric born in 1987.

Conformation
Identical to the Manx in every respect.

Coat
Thick and harsh long topcoat with an even thicker, woolly undercoat – described as very similar to that of the Norwegian Forest Cat.

Colours and Patterns
All colours and combinations of colours and patterns except that some associations do not accept cats with Siamese/Himalayan points pattern.

Eyes
Any colour in accordance with coat colour plus green, gold, copper, blue and odd eye colour (one eye blue and the other green, gold or copper) in whites.

Variation
Body conformation is virtually identical everywhere. Although this is required to be identical to that of the Manx the impression is sometimes given that the cat has a heavier build in colder climes. This is because of the heavier padding of its undercoat in colder areas. Judges are instructed to handle the cats thoroughly and not to judge breed type by sight alone.

Kittens
All Cymric kittens are born with the tail type they will retain throughout life – either no tail at all (rumpy); a tiny vestigate of tail made up of cartilege rather than bone (rumpy riser); a stump tail (stumpy); or an apparently normal tail (longy).

Personality
Confident and relaxed.

Voice
Reasonably quiet.

Show Status
Recognized for championship competition by the CCA and TICA; for registration and non-championship competition in other USA organizations and in Europe. Recognized for competition as a medallist breed by the Cat Association of Britain. Not eligible for competition in the British GCCF.

Breeding
Only Cymric, Manx, British Shorthair and Cymric or Manx variants are allowed in pedigrees for medallist status in Britain and pedigrees showing only Manx, Cymric and Manx and Cymric variants are preferred.

Black mackerel tabby Cymric

Javanese

Name
The only breed with four totally different names. Javanese reflects the closeness of the breed to the Balinese; also known as Oriental Longhair; Mandarin, and Angora. This last name is now only used by one of the two British associations. Known colloquially in Britain as Cuckoo cat.

Origins
When in her breeding programme involving Abyssinian/Siamese hybrids, Maureen Silson of the Southview cattery in Hertfordshire, England, produced cats with long hair. These were regarded as pets only; and when Southview Trappist was born in 1973 and developed a long chocolate-brown coat he was also considered to be a pet quality kitten. But as he grew it became apparent that his coat, rather unexpectedly, had nearly white roots. Maureen Silson began to suspect that he might be smoke and because she knew that Patricia Turner of the Scintilla cattery was researching the genetics of smokes she offered Trappist to her as a gift. The Scintilla household gave Trappist the domestic name of Cuckoo because among all the resident shorthairs he was the 'cuckoo in the nest'; and under this name he became famous in the cat fancy. Even now longhaired kittens of Oriental type are often known as Cuckoo cats and one club for the breed is actually named The Cuckoo Cat Club. Test matings to Scintilla Orientals in 1974 demonstrated that Trappist's light undercoat was different from that of smokes. In 1976 he was about to be neutered. However, some American visitors to the Scintilla cattery at this time spotted him and commented that he was similar to a Turkish Angora. This led Patricia Turner to research the Angora, as it has been known in Britain until the early twentieth century, and to publish a note in a cat fancy magazine inviting breeders interested in the re-creation of the Angora to contact her.

The possibility of importing Turkish Angoras was considered but it was known that the GCCF would not accept the documentary evidence supplied by the Ankhara Zoo; importing from the USA was too expensive. In any case none of the breeders involved was willing to inflict six months' isolation on imported cats or kittens. As a result a club was formed to re-create the original breed by selective breeding from Cuckoo. A breeding programme and a breed standard were drawn up.

For various reasons the Angora breeding programme proceeded at snail's pace for several years, and it was only when the Cat Association of Britain was formed in 1983 and granted it championship status that interest in the breed was aroused among members of the British public. In 1984 it was decided that the Turkish Angora and the Angora were two distinct breeds, that both should have championship status, and that the Angora should be improved to have true Oriental type. In October 1989 the CA decided that the use of the name Angora for an Oriental-type breed was confusing and that the name Javanese, already in use for Oriental Longhairs throughout all the member countries of FIFe, would be more appropriate. The fact that in the American CFA the breed name Javanese is used to define the red, tortie or tabby varieties of Balinese was not considered to be a valid reason against it.

In 1987 the Dutch breeders Ed and Helen van Kessel imported a blue Angora from Janet Pitman. This cat was given the breed name of Mandarin and later transferred to Inge and Johan van der Horst-Reckeeg of the Mi Lei-Fo cattery in Bovensmilde. There is now a small group of enthusiasts in the Netherlands. The breed is still in its infancy in the USA but at least one cat has been made up to Supreme Grand Champion.

Conformation
A graceful, elegant cat of slender Oriental build, long legs and a long wedged head with large ears. The tail is long enough to reach the point of the shoulder if measured along the length of the cat.

Coat
Very fine, soft and silky, longer on the tail, breeches and ruff and shorter on the sides and the head.

Colours
Black; blue; chocolate; cinnamon; lilac; fawn; red; cream and the tortie and silver varieties of those colours. *Note:* not all colours are recognized by all associations.

Patterns
Solid; tortoiseshell; smoke; ticked; mackerel; spotted and classic tabby; torbie.

Eyes
Bright green.

Personality
A sociable and charming cat, practised in the social graces.

Voice
Sometimes rather strident but conversationally moderate.

Kittens
Born with very fine soft hair which begins to become fluffy by the second or third week.

Show Status
First exhibited in Britain in 1974. Granted championship status by the CA of Britain in 1983 and in the USA by the ICA in 1985. Also a championship breed in all countries of FIFe and in most of the independent clubs of Europe. Not recognized for open class competition by the British GCCF. Bred and shown worldwide.

Breeding
Balinese, Siamese, Oriental Shorthairs are the only other breeds allowed within a three-generation pedigree.

Fawn Javanese

Maine Coon

Name
Thought to have acquired its name because tabby cats in the state of Maine had bushy striped tails resembling those of racoons. An alternative explanation is that the captain of an English trading ship whose name was Coon kept longhaired cats on board. Formerly known as American Longhair, Shag, or Maine trick cats.

Origins
In the late eighteenth century Maine was one of the largest ship-building states in the Union. Residents of the seaport towns were often masters of their own ships, taking their families with them on voyages overseas and bringing back a variety of animals and birds as pets, including cats, which fulfilled a double function as they were also ships' mousers. The Maine Coon undoubtedly evolved from backyard cats which descended from European cats taken on board these trading ships – including the longhaired cats of Scotland and Norway but also some Persians. Writing in *The Book of the Cat*, published in 1903, F. R. Pierce described his first Maine cat as a black pointed with white and known by the name of Captain Jenks of the Horse Marines.

By 1906 the CFA had twenty-eight Maine Coons registered in their studbook, but from that date on the popularity of the breed diminished. Largely due to the efforts of Ethelyn Whittemore of Maine and Ruby Dyer of Skowhegans the breed lines were maintained. In 1976 the breed was finally recognized by the CFA.

The first Maine Coon travelled to Europe in 1953 or 1954 when a female was taken to Austria from Canada and was later found to be pregnant. One of her kittens later became the first Maine Coon in Germany, where it was referred to as 'an American Forest Cat'.

In 1984 the Maine Coon came to Britain when Pat Brownsell of the Patriarca cattery imported Nephrani's Ashley and, later, Nephrani's Dexter bred by Ruth and Robert Morris in the USA.

Folklore
One legend claims that the cats descend from Norwegian Forest Cats sent to Maine by Marie Antoinette who was planning to escape there from the French Revolution. Another story is that New England sailors took home Angoras from Turkey in the late seventeenth century and that these cats interbred with the shorthaired domestics. Others believe the story of Captain Coon; and finally, some breeders used to believe that the cats descend from North American bobcats.

Conformation
Generally regarded as being a very large breed. The actual requirements for Maine Coon are 'medium to large' and breeders worry that judges and others may regard the biggest cats as the best. In fact, the Maine Coon should have a muscular broad-chested body which is long in relation to the strongly-boned legs so that the cat, if measured from withers to paws and withers to tail root, would fit into a rectangle. The wonderful Coon tail is long and should be so well furred that the coat flows. The head is medium in length and width and the muzzle, in mature cats, is rather square. The nose is of medium length and, in profile, slightly concave.

Coat
Heavy but with a silky texture, shorter on the shoulders and longer on the stomach and trousers. Ideally Coons have a ruff and bib of longer fur.

Colours
White; black; blue; red; cream; chinchilla; shaded silver; shell cameo; shaded cameo; black smoke; blue smoke; cameo smoke.

Patterns
Solid colours; classic (blotched); tabby; mackerel tabby; patched tabby (torbie); tortie; tortie and white; calico; dilute calico; blue cream; blue cream and white; bi-colour; smoke.

Eyes
Shades of green, gold or copper with golden, blue or one eye golden and the other blue in whites.

Variation
Muzzle shape develops slowly and may not be at its full squareness until the cat is over two years old. Females may not develop as much squareness of muzzle. During the hottest months the cat may lose most of its ruff and trousers.

Personality
Independent, playful and full of energy.

Voice
Moderate.

Kittens
Kittens develop quite slowly and their coats vary in accordance with colour. From about seven days of age the eyelids open to reveal baby blue eyes which gradually change to green or gold as the kitten grows.

Show Status
Recognized for championships in virtually all associations except the GCCF of Britain. Shown worldwide.

Breeding
Only Maine Coons are allowed in pedigrees in CFA. Other US associations permit the introduction of unregistered Coons. In the countries of FIFe only Maine Coons are allowed in the full register although cats winning in Novice classes may be given a 'control' pedigree. In the independent clubs of Europe unregistered Maine Coon-type cats may be entered as Maine Coon if they are successful in a Determination class. In Britain, in both GCCF and CA only Maine Coons are allowed in Maine Coon pedigrees.

Black classic tabby Maine Coon

Norwegian Forest Cat

Name
The name denotes the origin of the breed in the forests of Norway. Norwegian Forest Cat (English); Chat de Bois Norvégian (French); Norwegische Waldkatze (German); Skogkatt or Norsk Skogkatt, formerly Trollkatt (Norwegian). Known colloquially as the Wegi.

Origins
The similarity between the Maine Coon and the Norwegian Forest Cat and of both of them to the Scottish wildcat suggests that they have a common origin, and that the link between the three was the Viking ships which carried domesticated cats on board and visited the shores of North America and Scotland. Another theory is that Angora cats taken from Iran to Italy in 1521 arrived at Norwegian ports as ships' cats and then mated with native shorthairs in their new country. Finally, others suggest that the breed derives from shorthair British domestic cats and longhaired cats brought back by the Crusaders. What is certain is that Norwegian Forest Cats have existed in Norway 'for as long as anyone can remember'.

Despite their pride in their native cat the Norwegians did not consider it worthy of exhibition until the 1930s when a group of Norwegian fanciers commenced a breeding campaign. From about 1963 Wegies were entered in shows under the name Skogkatt and in 1972 the Norwegian Forest Cat was recognized, with a provisional standard, by the independent clubs of Norway. In 1973 Edel Runas, Else Nylund and her family formulated a breeding programme. Many of the cats they used were found near the Swedish border; and this led to the suggestion by Swedish breeders that the breed belonged to Sweden as much as to Norway. But the Norwegians fought off the Swedes: it was agreed that foundation cats must come 'straight from the Norwegian forests'. It was decided that although single Skogkatts might cross the Swedish/Danish border while hunting in the woods no entire registered cats should be allowed out of the country until the breed was recognized.

In 1977 the Norwegian Forest Cat was proclaimed a championship breed in all the countries of FIFe and history had been made.

The first exports were to the Netherlands, to members of the Dutch club Mundikat. Subsequently exports were made to Sweden, Germany, Finland, Denmark, Italy, France and the USA. British breeders imported Norwegian Forest Cats only recently and a club was formed in 1987.

Breeders in the USA felt a particular affinity with the Norwegian Forest Cat, probably because of its resemblance to the Maine Coon. By the end of 1985 there were 134 Norwegian Forest Cats in the USA.

Folklore
Norse mythology tells of a cat so large that the thunder god Thor could not lift it off the ground. Freya, the goddess of love and fertility, is said to have ridden in a chariot drawn by two such cats. Norwegian fairytales mention troll cats which were huge and furry.

Conformation
A large, solidly-built breed with muscles which may not be fully developed until the cat is nearly five years old. The head is unique among the semi-longhaired breeds as its shape forms an equilateral triangle in space with large, tufted ears set so that their outer edges are in line with the lines of the face. Seen from the side the nose is straight. The chin is strong but the muzzle is gently rounded rather than being square as in the Maine Coon. The tail is long and very well covered with fur.

Coat
A glossy, hard-textured, water-repellent topcoat covers a dense, more woolly undercoat so that the cat has protection in wet and cold weather conditions. In full coat the cat is magnificent, with a full ruff and brisket, long 'knickerbockers' and a bushy tail.

Colours
All colours are accepted other than Siamese pointing and the chocolate and lilac colours, although black tabbies and black and white tabbies seem to be the most popular outside Norway. In its native land the most popular variety is black and white.

Patterns
All patterns are allowed other than Siamese pointing.

Eyes
All colours are acceptable.

Personality
Viking cats – adventurous and with a prediliction for looting, yet still making loving, adaptable pets.

Voice
Moderately conversational with soft tones.

Kittens
Born shorthaired and the fluffiness develops in the first few. Kitten coat is soft and the tough guard hair texture develops as the kitten matures.

Show Status
Recognized for championships in all countries of FIFe; by TICA, CFF and ACFA in the USA; and by the CA of Britain. Also bred by breeders of the CFA in the USA (but without championship status), and by British breeders in the GCCF without competitive open class or championship status.

Breeding
Only Norwegian Forest Cats are allowed in pedigrees although cats with unregistered Norwegian Forest Cats within three generations are acceptable in most USA clubs and the CA of Britain if the foundation cats have been accepted by FIFe's Norwegian registry.

Black and white Norwegian Forest Cat

Ragdoll

Name
Named because of its habit of relaxing when handled, like a ragdoll.

Origins
The Ragdoll originated comparatively recently in the USA from matings between a white longhaired female cat owned by Ann Baker and a Birman male. The litter included two cats which their owner named Raggedy Ann Daddy Warbucks and Raggedy Ann Gueber.

Ann Baker took a decision to franchise her cats so that purchasers were not free to breed under their own catteries or without additional payment and her consent. Despite this restriction the NCFA accepted the Ragdoll as a breed for registration in 1965. Some of the early cats had no white markings and their variety was called Colourpoint. Others had white feet, a white chin, chest and belly and this pattern became known as 'mitted'. It soon became clear that when mitted was mated to mitted some of the kittens produced had much more white than either parent. This third white spotting pattern became known as Bi-Colour. However the NCFA refused recognition to anything other than the mitted variety.

When Denny Dayton and his wife of the Blossom-Time cattery in California purchased cats from Ann Baker they began a long campaign to get the breed on to a sound genetic footing and to gain wider recognition. In time their work resulted in championship status in nearly all the USA registries and most of the popularity and success the breed enjoys today can be credited to them.

In September 1981 the Ragdolls came to Britain when Lulu Rowley of the Petil-Lu cattery in Norwich purchased four cats from the Daytons. In 1983 she was able to compete with her cats at the first CA show, held at the Sandown Park Racecourse in Surrey.

Today the Ragdoll is a popular breed in Britain as well as in the USA and is catered for internationally by the Ragdoll Fanciers club as well as by the National Ragdoll Cat Association in the CA and the British Ragdoll Cat Association in the GCCF.

Lulu Rowley and Pat Brownsell both exported Ragdolls to mainland Europe and other breeders there purchased stock directly from the USA.

Folklore
Alleged to have an abnormally high tolerance to pain, to lack fear and to go limp when handled as a result of an injury in a traffic accident sustained by the founder white queen. Although this story is folklore it held back worldwide recognition of the breed in some associations until laboratory and veterinary tests demonstrated the breed to be a variety of normal cat.

Conformation
A large breed with a long body, strong legs, large paws and a mobile, well furred long tail. The head is broad between the ears as in the Birman and the Persian and seen in profile the forehead slopes down to a rounded chin with a slight indent (often described as being like a ski-slope) between the eyes. Unlike other breeds the Ragdoll is allowed by its standards to own a loose fatty area on the belly.

Coat
A silky thick coat of medium length which has a shorter, still silky undercoat which, when well groomed looks magnificent, producing breeches, ruff and a full plumed tail.

Colours
Seal point, blue point, chocolate point and lilac point in all countries. Red point, cream point, seal tortie point, blue tortie point, chocolate tortie point and lilac tortie point in Britain only.

Patterns
Colourpoint: Pointed as in the Colourpoint/Himalayan, with no white areas.
Mitted: Pointed as in the Colourpoint Ragdoll but with the addition of white mittens on all four legs, a white band running from the chin right down the belly to the undertail and a white chin. Some societies also allow a white inverted 'V' on the mask.
Bi-Colour: Pointed as in the Colourpoint Ragdoll with all four legs, the chin, chest, belly and an inverted V on the muzzle white. Some cats have a white area centrally down the back but this is not faulted by judges. Great importance is placed upon symmetry of the inverted V on the face.

Eyes
Bright china blue.

Personality
A cat well known for its 'laid back' personality.

Voice
Moderate.

Kittens
Born white or nearly white and the coloured points begin to develop when the kitten is about a week old. The coat may continue to develop shading, which tones with the points until it is fully mature. The points density should then remain the same but the degree of shading will vary with the seasons of the year. A breed that is notoriously slow to mature.

Show Status
Recognized for championship competition in 1975 in North America in ACA, ACC, ACFA, CFF, NCFA, TICA and UCF and accepted for registration by CFA. Recognized for championships in Britain by the CA in 1983. Eligible for competition as an unrecognized longhair breed in all countries of the FIFe. Not eligible for competition in breed classes in the GCCF

Breeding
Only Ragdolls are allowed in pedigrees for championship competition.

Seychellois Longhair

Name
So named because the coat patterns of coloured tail and white body with dashes and splashes of colour on the body are those known genetically as the Seychelles patterns.

Origins
While reading reports on cat gene surveys in the late 1970s Patricia Turner of the Scintilla cattery in Milton Keynes, England, became inspired by a wish to re-create the coat patterns reported by Professor Paul Jaffe in his study of the cats of the Seychelles. This became possible in 1984 when she acquired two Persian cats – both tortie and white – which became the foundation cats of the new breed. One stayed at the Scintilla cattery and the other went to Julie Smith's Dovetrees cattery. As the generation numbers advanced the breeding programme evolved towards a Seychelles-patterned cat of Oriental body type and Siamese blue eyes. The foundation females were Patricia Turner's Snowdrop Gentle Pedilase and Julie Smith's Dovetrees Tarantella and the foundation males were Scintilla Pastelle Royale and Champion Scintilla Caramellian of Jamais. Both males were Siamese. Progeny from matings between these four cats were backcrossed to Siamese and Oriental mates and their progeny were mated like to like to achieve the Seychelles coat pattern. The programme is still continuing and in some lines the fifth generation has been reached. The first Seychelles-patterned cats in the programme were Scintilla Félicité, Scintilla Amirante, Scintilla Victoria and Scintilla Thérèse. Fécilité and Victoria were the first of the breed to be exhibited. In 1989 the Seychellois Cat Society was formed with a founder membership of Derek and Pauline Parsons of the Shalimar cattery, Maureen Trompetto of the Lincret cattery, John Mais of the Jamais cattery, Shirley Mizon of the Zelstone cattery and Patricia Turner. Current emphasis upon the breeding of variants by mating back to Siamese in order to improve type rather than on breeding larger numbers of cats eligible for the show bench. Variants are cats of Seychellois breeding but with too much colour for the Seychelles patterns.

Conformation
Svelte, long-bodied and elegant with long slim legs, a long whippy tail and a long, wedged head crowned by large wide-set ears and with slanting Oriental eyes. The whip tail, if measured along the body, should reach the point of the shoulder.

Coat
Long, fine, close-lying and silky with plumed tail.

Colours
White with any colour or combination of colours except black.

Patterns
Mainly white with coloured dashes and splashes of colour occurring randomly on the head, legs and body but always with coloured tails. The patterns are defined as Seychellois Septième (relatively large splashes and dashes of colour on the flanks, legs and head and coloured tail); Seychellois Huitième (the coloured areas appreciably smaller but still present on the flanks, head, legs and coloured tail); and Seychellois Neuvième (the coloured areas small and confined to the head and legs with a coloured tail).

Eyes
Brilliant blue.

Personality
Scatterbrained, demonstrative and demanding of human attention at all times. Very athletic.

Voice
Garrulous but musical.

Kittens
Born pure nearly white and the colour develops slowly. In red, cream, apricot and their tortie varieties the full expression of the coloured areas may not be apparent until the cat is three years old so that categorizing into Septième, Huitième or Neuvième may be very difficult until that time. Longhairs look the same as the shorthairs for the first few weeks. The fluffy coat only begins to grow fluffy from about the second week.

Show Status
First exhibited in 1988 at a CA of Britain show in Newbury, Berkshire, and subsequently at other CA of Britain shows. Accepted by the CA as a provisional breed without championship status, it is also eligible for competition in non-championship classes at shows of the FIFe. Currently all Seychellois breeders are in Britain.

Breeding
The CA of Britain requires that pedigrees may include cats of Siamese conformation only.

Blue tortoiseshell Seychellois neuvieme

Siberian

Name
The name refers to the breed's origins in the Soviet Union.

Origins
Cats would have entered Russia from Europe, by land and sea, from Persia by overland trade routes and from the Far East via the sea ports and trading vessels. The influence of the Far East is proved by the high proportion of kinky-tailed cats in the eastern Soviet Union, this characteristic being common in Japan and South East Asia. Other studies have revealed that the cat populations in Euro-Russia and Siberia remain much as they were in medieval, or even earlier, times.

The world wide census of cat coat colours and coat length which has now been in progress for over two decades has revealed that the mutant for long hair must have occurred in Russia many centuries ago and that it spread first to Turkey and Persia. It therefore seems reasonable that the Persian, evolved from longhair cats of Persia, and the Angora, evolved from longhair cats of Turkey, both have their origins in the Siberian. In fact it seems that all longhair breeds obtained that characteristic from the cats of Russia, and that while they have been refined into a number of specialist breeds their founder breed – the Siberians – have been unknown outside the USSR until comparatively recently.

There are clear similarities between the Siberian and the Norwegian Forest Cat and Maine Coon, and just as it may reasonably be conjectured that the last two have a common origin so may it be concluded that this is shared with the Siberian and that the Siberian is the ancestor of them both.

The reasons for the success of the longhair gene in Russia are not known but it has been suggested that it was due either to a favourable environment or because regional factors encouraged a rapid increase in frequency. A number of Russian geneticists, notably P. Borodin, M. Bochkarev, M. Smirnova and P. Manchenko are now studying domestic cat populations in the USSR and work already completed has revealed that the longhair gene is found at a very high frequency right across from Leningrad, where it is 64 per cent, to Khabarovsk on the east coast above Korea, where it is 21 per cent.

In addition the USSR possesses wildcats, *Felis silvestris*, which mate with domestic cats, particularly in rural areas; and the introduction of the wild-type genes would decrease the level of mutant genes such as non-agouti and blue. In areas where such matings may have occurred regularly the Siberian will occur more frequently with a tabby pattern.

From the moment when the cat fancy of the USSR began to gain momentum the rare prize in its midst was treasured and several cat clubs now plan breeding programmes.

Conformation
A sturdily built cat with a relatively long body and strong legs. The head is broad across the skull and rounder than in the Maine Coon or Norwegian Forest Cat. The full tail reaches nearly to the shoulders.

Coat
Long, with a glossy layer of top coat and a densely padded thick insulating undercoat with the longest areas at the ruff, breeches and tail.

Colours and Patterns
Reported to be under development in a wide range of colours but best known for the golden tabby variety where the basic tabby pattern is black with the base of the hairs and the undercoat of golden agouti.

Eyes
In keeping with the coat colour. In the golden tabby the eye colour is hazel to green.

Personality
Docile and relaxed.

Voice
Quiet: similar to the Persian.

Kittens
The coat is short at birth, growing longer week by week so that by four weeks of age the kittens are decidedly fluffy and by three months the glossy top coat of guard hairs is developing. Golden tabbies are born much darker than they will be in maturity.

Show Status
Not yet a championship breed in the FIFe countries but eligible for competition in classes for unrecognized breeds. Show status in the independent associations not yet decided. The breed has not been shown outside the USSR.

Breeding
Only Siberians allowed in pedigrees, although not all Siberians have registered pedigrees.

Golden mackerel tabby Siberian

Somali

Name
Named after Somalia, which borders Abyssinia (now Ethiopia), in order to record the similarity between the Somali and its parent breed, the Abyssinian.

Origins
Longhaired kittens sometimes occurred in Abyssinian litters in Britain, the USA, Canada, Australia and New Zealand from the time proper records were kept. They were known as 'sports' and were usually sold to people who would keep the secret of their ancestry. Most of the Abyssinians in these countries traced their ancestry to cats exported from Britain and breeders researching pedigrees have found that most Somalis have pedigrees going back to British exports. One such cat was Raby Chuffa, who was bred by Lady Barnard, and sent to the USA in 1952. It was not until 1967 that Evelyn Mague, a breeder in New Jersey, USA, having unexpectedly bred a longhaired Abyssinian from a mating between two normal-coated Abyssinians realized that she had the prototype for a new breed. She named the kitten George and set about repeating the mating with a view to producing sufficient breeding stock to start a formal breeding programme.

In continental Europe the first Somalis were imported from the USA in 1977, but longhairs had cropped up in Abyssinian litters in several European countries before that date. In Australia and New Zealand breeders had formed a special breeders group to develop their own line of Somalis and it is recorded that a Somali was exhibited in Australia as early as 1965.

In Britain the occurrence of longhaired kittens in Abyssinian lines was generally a well-kept secret until Mrs McLaughlin exhibited a litter of six kittens from an Abyssinian queen at the 1971 Kensington Kitten and Neuter Cat Club Show. All the kittens were sorrel, four were normal short-coated Abyssinians and the other two were longhaired. Fellow breeders were not pleased with Mrs McLaughlin, but her courageous action did result in pedigree research which allowed breeders to determine which cats might be the longhair carriers. The difference between the outlook of British, Australian and American breeders was revealed when, instead of nurturing the longhair Abyssinian to form a new breed as the latter had done, all effort in Britain was put into clamping down on the pedigrees in which the longhair gene was present.

It was only in 1982, when the Somali had become 'respectable', that the British realized how attractive the cat could be and imports from the USA were made to start a breeding programme.

Conformation
A twin to the Abyssinian in every respect other than coat, the Somali shares the 'neither cobby nor Oriental' breed type. The face is not as round as in the British Shorthair, nor as pointed as in the Siamese. In fact the top of the head and down the sides of the face should almost fit into a perfect equilateral triangle, although all head contours are rounded. The ears are placed so that their outer edges follow the same lines as the line of the face and muzzle. Legs are fairly long in proportion to the body and the feet have an oval shape. The tail is long and fairly thick at the base.

Coat
The beautiful Somali coat is composed of long, very fine, densely-packed hairs. It has a full ruff, breeches and brush (the coat on the tail), the coat on the head being short and on the rest of the body medium length.

Colours
Ruddy; blue; chocolate; sorrel; lilac; fawn; all these colours in tortie; red; cream and all these colours in silver.

Patterns
All over agouti with slightly darker shading along the spine and down the tail, dark heels and dark eye liner. Each hair is ticked and banded alternately light and dark and the clarity and number of bands are of prime importance. In full coat some exhibition Somalis have about fourteen bands in one hair. Some cats have greyish colouration at the roots of the hair but this is regarded as a fault, as is reverse ticking, where the tip of the hair is the lighter colour.

Eyes
Gold or green in North America. Amber, green or yellow in most other cat fancy organizations.

Variation
The differences in conformation between the Somali of Europe and the Somali of North America reflect the differences between the Abyssinian in these countries. Not all associations recognize all Somali colours.

Personality
Extrovert with a 'come-and-look-at-me' personality.

Voice
Vocal but not noisy.

Kittens
Born much darker overall and the lighter agouti ticking and banding becomes evident only as the kitten develops. The coat appears short in the first week, gradually becoming fluffy and then, at the age of three or four months, attains the smooth silky texture desired in the adult cat.

Show Status
Recognized for championships in the USA in 1979; in some independent clubs of Europe in 1980; in the countries of FIFe in 1982. A championship breed in Britain since 1983 in the CA. Not recognized by the British GCCF.

Breeding
Only Somalis and Abyssinians allowed within three generations.

Turkish Angora

Name
Named after the capital city of Turkey. The name of the city was changed to Ankara in 1930 but the animal breeds of Turkey, famous for their long silky coats, retained the ancient name. Formerly known simply as Angora.

Origins
The Turkish Angora is an ancient breed which was recognized by the cat fancy from the start, then lost, and recognized again 100 years later. As early as the sixteenth century Turkey was famous for its Angora cats. Historians differ on the date when the Angora was first taken to Europe but by the early seventeenth century the breed had spread to Italy, France and Britain. In 1868 it was described as 'a beautiful variety with silvery hair of fine texture, generally longest on the neck but also in the tail', and in 1889 Harrison Weir commented: 'The best are of high value, a pure white with blue eyes, being thought the perfection of cats, all other points being good, and its hearing by no means defective . . . The colours are varied but the black which should have orange eyes, as should the slate colours, and blues, and the whites are the most esteemed.'

From Europe the Angora travelled to America but there it was bred together with the Persians and the true Angora was lost. In Turkey the government set up a selective breeding programme at the Ankara Zoo because the breed was in danger of becoming extinct. In the early 1960s two unrelated Angoras – an odd-eyed male named Yildiz (meaning star) and an amber-eyed female named Yildizcik (startlet) – were purchased by US breeders and registered with the CFA as Longhairs and in March 1963 their first litter was born. Two kittens were retained for breeding, named Mustapha and Suna Aisha. Mustapha, the male, had one blue eye and one amber while Suna Aisha had amber eyes. Further cats were imported and within two years there were twelve or more Angora breeders in the USA.

At the annual meeting of the CFA in 1967 three Turkish Angora cats were presented and the following year CFA began to register them as Angora rather than simply as Longhair. Other breeders imported directly from the zoo at Ankara and towards the end of the 1960s The Original Turkish Angora Society was formed. At first only white Angoras were considered because white was the only colour preserved by Ankara Zoo. However in 1978 the CFA acknowledged that colours could occur and the establishment of breeding lines for specific colours began.

Turkish Angora were also imported directly from Turkey to Sweden and to Britain. In about 1977 an American Air Force Captain named Sharon Thomas purchased a pair from Ankara Zoo and took them with her to her air force station in Britain. A male from the resultant litter was owned by a British Angora breeder – Carol Andrews of the Ohope cattery – for many years and his descendants are still breeding.

The true Turkish Angora is now established in many European countries, and although many colours are bred white remains the most popular.

Folklore
It was believed in Turkey that Ataturk would return in the guise of a deaf white Angora cat.

Conformation
A medium-sized cat with rather long body and relatively light bone structure. Legs quite long and paws small and round with tufts of long hair between the toes. The head is small in relation to the body and is plumed with long silky hair.

Coat
Medium long on the body but longer on the ruff and tail. Very fine and silky in texture.

Colours
White; black; cream; red; in tabbies, silver tabby.

Patterns
None in solid colours but among the coloured varieties all tabby patterns, tortoiseshells, tortoiseshell and whites, bi-colours and smokes are allowed.

Eyes
Blue, amber or, in white cats, one eye blue and the other amber. Amber in all colours other than in silver tabby when it is green or hazel.

Variation
The coat may become virtually shorthaired except on the tail during the summer months.

Personality
Responsive, intelligent and alert.

Voice
Tuneful but not over loud.

Kittens
Born with silky coats. The long coat gradually develops as the weeks go by.

Show Status
Recognized for championship status by CFA in the USA: for championship status in Britain by the CA, and in all countries of FIFe. Not recognised by Britain's GCCF. Bred and shown worldwide.

Breeding
Only Turkish Angoras are allowed in pedigrees.

Blue-eyed white Turkish Angora

Turkish Van

Name
Named after the area of Lake Van in Turkey where it originated. At first it was known as the Van Cat. This was amended to Turkish Cats for the purposes of recognition in Britain. In recent years the name Turkish Van has become widely used, although the GCCF still refers to the cat as Turkish. Once publicized as the Turkish swimming cat.

Origins
Longhaired white cats with orange auburn tails have been domesticated for centuries in the Lake Van area of south-eastern Turkey and they are prized as pets. In 1955 when the British photographers Laura Lushington and Sonya Halliday travelled to the area they were amazed and delighted by the gift of two Van kittens. Local people explained that the cats had a reputation for enjoying a bath in the warm shallow pools of the area.

The kittens were named Van Attala (male) and Van Guzelli Iskenderun (female). They travelled with the two photographers until their assignment was completed and then went into the six month's quarantine required by the British authorities for all imported cats. Subsequently, as fully grown cats, they joined Laura Lushington at her cottage in Weston Turville, Buckinghamshire, England. On subsequent trips to Turkey three more white cats with auburn tails were located, acquired and put into quarantine. Because there was no cat fancy in Turkey no formal pedigree records of the cats had been kept in their native land and, although the British GCCF was provided with documents from the Turkish embassy stating that the cats represented a natural Turkish breed, they insisted that the cats be bred and registered for at least four generations before they would consider admitting them. The GCCF did agree to register them as 'Any Other Colour' and Laura Lushington, aided by her friend, then set about the establishment of a Turkish cat family in England large enough to avoid excessive inbreeding and to provide the required four generations of ancestors for breed recognition. While doing so they achieved a great deal of publicity for the breed by supplying photographs of the cats swimming in streams in their native Turkey and in the bath at the cottage.

They began to advertise the kittens for sale and to exhibit the cats at shows. Unfortunately the advertisements nearly lost the breed its chance of recognition because the cats were described as 'Van Cats' and Van had been registered by Laura Lushington as her cattery name. Additionally the advertisements stated that Laura Lushington was the sole breeder in Britain. (The GCCF refuses to grant recognition to a cat bred by an owner who has its name as her registered cattery name and claims sole rights as breeder.)

At the suggestion of Patricia Turner, then secretary to the GCCF club catering for new breeds, a proposed breed standard was compiled, registration certificates were collated, the proposed breed name was amended to Turkish and the policy of restricting the breeding to one cattery was abandoned. A number of other breeders became involved, notably Lydia Russell of the Kastamonou cattery. The club sponsored the re-application and recognition of the breed under the name of Turkish was granted in 1969.

The breed was recognized for championship by FIFe in 1971, the year after the founder male Van Attala died at fifteen years of age.

Conformation
A long-proportioned sturdy body set on strong legs with round, tufted paws and a full-coated, medium-length tail. The head shows a short muzzle in relation to the whole foreface with large ears, 'feathered' with long hair. Although sometimes compared to the Turkish Angora, the Van is actually a much heavier breed.

Coat
Long and silky without and woolly undercoat.

Colours
Chalky white and auburn red; chalky white and cream; chalky white and black tortoiseshell; chalky white and blue cream. Not all colours are recognized by all associations. The auburn red or cream areas may show faint tabby ringing.

Patterns
The pattern known to geneticists as Grade 8 or 9 piebald or, more poetically, as one of the Seychelles patterns. However the cat fancy usually refers to this degree of white marking as 'Van pattern'.

Eyes
Usually amber, although some cats have blue eyes and others have one eye amber and the other blue.

Variation
Coat varies with the seasons so that in the summer months the cat may appear to be nearly short-coated.

Personality
Home-loving and adaptable, although sometimes self-opinionated when meeting judges at shows.

Voice
Melodious. Described as 'like little bells'.

Kittens
Kittens are born with slightly fluffy coats and the longer hair develops gradually through kittenhood.

Show Status
First exhibited in Britain in the later 1950s. Recognized for championship competition in Britain in 1969 and in the member countries of FIFe in 1971.

Breeding
Only Turkish Van are allowed in Turkish Van pedigrees.

Auburn and white Turkish Van

The Rex Group

Coats which have a decided waviness are known as rexed and there are three separate rexed breeds already recognized by the cat fancy. These are the Cornish Rex, developed from a wavy-coated cat found in Cornwall, England; the Devon Rex, developed from a wavy-coated cat found in Devon, England; and the German Rex, developed from a wavy-coated cat found in East Germany. Although the German Rex probably mutated before the other two it is now exceedingly rare, even in Germany, and does not have a separate entry here.

These three breeds do not represent the only occurrences of rex. A rex cat was described in Germany in 1931, in the USA in 1937, in Italy in 1950 and in the USA again in 1952, 1959 and 1960. None of these was developed into breeds, probably because they were not sufficiently different from the existing three to allow for cat fancy recognition.

The hair of a normal cat consists of three different types – the stout, primary guard hairs (top coat); the slightly thinner secondary guard hairs or 'awn' hairs; and the down hairs which are the most numerous and shorter than both other types. The guard hairs are the longest hairs in the cat's coat; they are always straight and they taper to a spear-like tip, whereas the down hairs are extremely fine and of uniform thickness from root to tip. The down hairs make up the bulk of the coat, providing insulation from extremes of temperature, and they are 'guarded' by the top layer of coarser hair. The natural straightness and strength of the guard hairs prevent the finer down hair from waving, except on areas such as the belly where the hair is mostly down and where waviness frequently occurs, even in non-rexed breeds.

In the Cornish Rex coat the primary guard hairs are missing, leaving only the secondary guard hairs, which are less strong and coarse, to protect the down hair. Both the secondary guard hairs and the down hairs are shorter than normal and both are wavy. Whiskers are shorter and bent and very brittle. The Devon Rex coat is slightly different as both types of guard hair and the down hair are present, although all three tend to be more abnormally bent than in the Cornish. The Devon Rex's whiskers are reduced to a vestigial length and are twisted, bent and easily broken. The Devon Rex has a tendency to shed a great deal of hair when moulting and bare areas are common on the shoulders, chest, belly, on the top of the head and around the neck.

Grooming the rexes is quite an art. The Devon coat tends to feel coarser and firmer than that of the Cornish, which can be described as silky. Although the hair of the Devon is generally shorter than that of the Cornish there is considerable variation from the longest hairs to the shortest hairs in each cat, and between texture in different coat colours. The wave pattern of the Devon coat fits the cat's personality, for both are slightly disorderly! In fact one Devon rex was registered with the name Druncandisorderly!

It is necessary to stroke the Devon coat quite hard in order to show the waviness at its best. The waviness is usually most apparent on the back and sides of the cat and least apparent on the belly, top of head and haunches. Devon coats, if too long, look shaggy, and without regular grooming they can often get rather greasy. Before a show it is wisest to give a bran bath to remove excess oil. Devons have a tendency to grow wiry coarse coat along the line of the spine, and this can be corrected by regular application of

wheatgerm or rape seed oil during the weeks when the cat is not going to a show. If the cat licks its coat it will come to no harm and once the oiliness is removed by washing that area with a Ph balanced skin wash the once wiry hair will be soft. Judges consider it important for the Devon to be fully coated and marks are lost for bare patches. Extensive baldness may lead to disqualification.

The Cornish coat needs slightly different care. It should be as dense and silky as possible and any tendency to shagginess is regarded as a fault. Hand grooming enhances the regular marcel wavy pattern, but care must be taken not to make the coat over-greasy as a result. Depending on coat colour exhibitors use very fine powder dry shampoos on the cat's coat and on their hands while hand grooming. Bran baths are ideal for the show preparation of most Cornish Rexes.

Rexes are particularly prone to a condition known as stud tail. The name is misleading since the condition is seen in both sexes. It results from a build-up of excess sebum which blocks the pores of the skin on the upper surface of the tail, near to the root. Regular attention to the tail is advised and this involves washing the area with a facial shampoo brush or a soft shaving brush and a Ph balanced anti-bacterial wash for greasy skins. If the pores become completely blocked blackheads will form, the hair will become discoloured and fall out and the skin may become red, swollen and inflamed. If this happens veterinary advice is needed.

Cornish Rex

Name

The name refers to the origin of the breed in Cornwall, England. In the early days of the breed it was known as Gene 1 Rex.

Origins

The first Cornish Rex was born on 21 July 1950 at a farm on Bodmin Moor, Cornwall, England, in a litter of five. The queen was Serena, a tortie and white shorthair domestic cat owned by Nina Ennismore. As the kitten grew it became more and more obvious that he was different to his littermates, with a slender body, a whippy tail, a wedge-shaped head, a wavy red and white coat and curly whiskers. He was named Kallibunker. On the advice of her veterinary surgeon Nina Ennismore contacted A. C. Jude, a mouse breeder with a particular interest in the newly discovered rex varieties. He suggested a programme of inbreeding from kittens bred from Kallibunker mated back to Serena. Nina Ennismore followed his instructions and between 1950 and 1956 her cattery grew to forty cats, most of them rexes. In 1956 she called a halt and began to have the majority of her cats, including Serena and Kallibunker, put to sleep. She had attempted to sell some of them but became disillusioned over the fact that her valuation of her cats was far higher than that of potential buyers. However, a small circle of cat fancy breeders did take an interest, notably Brian Stirling-Webb of the famous Briarry cattery. He purchased an entire male named Poldhu who, before he left Nina Ennismore, had mated a blue female named Lamorna Cove.

Nina Ennismore loaned her cream and white half-brother of Lamorna Cove, Sham Pain Chas, to Brian Stirling-Webb in order that the British breeding programme could commence. Chas was mated to Burmese and British shorthairs and as a result the rexes produced in the second generation became far cobbier and stockier than before. Lamorna Cove was sent while in kitten to Frances Blancheri in the USA in 1957, and her two blue and white kittens named Diamond Lil and Marmaduke became the founder cats of the American Cornish Rex breed. Marmaduke's owner, Helen Weiss, was concerned about the amount of inbreeding in the pedigree and outcrossed to Siamese. Her decision to use Siamese as the outcross breed resulted in the emergence of the elegant, fine-boned breed it is today. With the success of the US outcrosses to Siamese came the realization in Britain that the use of Burmese and British shorthairs had lost the original finer type of the breed and so steps were taken for the purchase of a fine-boned male (Rio Vista Kismet) who was a great-great-great-grandson of Kallibunker. Since then other British breeders have purchased American-type Cornish Rex so that although there still remains a difference between the two groups that difference is significantly less than it was some years ago. Some differences, particularly those of leg length and head type, are likely to remain because of differences in the breed standard requirements in the USA and Europe.

Conformation

The greyhound of the cat fancy, the Cornish Rex is fine-boned and elegant with long legs, slender body and a whipped tail. The back has a natural arch with the lower line of the body curving upward to give a greyhound-like 'tuck-up'. The arch is most evident when the cat is standing. The head is somewhat narrow with a profile composed of two convex arcs, and the forehead rounded leading to a high-bridged nose, thus producing a Roman profile. The ears are large and set high on the head.

Coat

A short and plushy-textured coat resulting from a recessive gene which produces hair half the normal length and lacking in primary guard hairs. Secondary guard hairs – otherwise known as awn hairs – are present but are modified to become almost indistinguishable from the soft down hairs (the undercoat). As primary guard hairs are straight and relatively coarse their absence, combined with the lessened length and strength of the secondary guard hairs, allows the down hairs to wave. As a result the rex coat shows waving throughout the body, particularly on the back. Whiskers and eyebrows are curly.

Colours and Patterns

All colours, patterns and colour and pattern combinations, although some associations do not accept the combination of white with Siamese pattern.

Eyes

All colours in keeping with coat colour.

Variation

Variation in coat colour at the time of the moult is less noticeable than in other breeds due to the absence of guard hairs in the coat. The degree of wave varies with age, nutritional and hormonal status.

Personality

Very agile. A feline comedian.

Voice

Quiet.

Kittens

Kittens open their eyes at about five days. Ears begin to open at about two weeks. Most kittens are born very wavy. The wave usually diminishes at about five to six weeks, regaining its quality gradually as the kitten grows.

Show Status

First exhibited in London at the Kensington Kitten and Neuter Cat Club Show. First recognized for championship competition in the USA by the UCF and later by the CFA in 1964. Recognized in Britain in 1967. Siamese-pattern Cornish Rex recognized for championship competition in the CFA of the USA in 1986. Now a championship breed worldwide.

Blue Cornish Rex

Devon Rex

Name
The name is derived from the county of the breed's origin in England. In the early years of the breed it was known as Gene 2 Rex.

Origins
In 1960 a tortie and white ex-stray female cat living under the protection of Beryl Cox of Buckfastleigh, Devon, gave birth to kittens in the field next to the house. The litter included a dusty black curly-coated male. It was soon realized that the sire must be the strange curly-coated tomcat sometimes seen in the locality of a local disused tin mine. Beryl Cox kept the kitten and named him Kirlee. He became a much-loved pet; and when she read of the Cornish Rex in a newspaper report of 1961 she contacted Brian Stirling-Webb with details. He persuaded her to let him have Kirlee in the belief that he would be of value in the Cornish Rex breeding programme and with regret she did so. In due course Kirlee was mated to the rex descendants of Kallibunker but all the kittens were normal-coated. It became obvious that Kirlee was of a different type of gene complex from Kallibunker and a programme of inbreeding was commenced in order to preserve and develop this second type of rex. By this time Kirlee's dam had died so he was mated to his normal-coated daughters. Eventually a breeding population of the Gene 2 Rex was built up and standards were drawn up for recognition as a championship breed. The breed journeyed to the USA where a breeding programme started in 1968.

Conformation
Short head with low-set, wide-based ears, giving a pixie look. The body is somewhat tubular with a level topline and virtually no 'tuck-up'. The tail is long, fine and tapering and the medium-length legs are fine-boned, though not as fine as in the Cornish Rex.

Coat
A very short and fragile coat with a rippled wave resulting from a recessive gene which retards hair growth. All three hair types are present, but are changed so much that they almost resemble down hairs, thus producing waviness, an effect which becomes more apparent when smoothed with the hand. The Devon Rex coat has less density overall than the Cornish Rex. The guard hairs are sometimes noticeably coarse and harsh on the back. Whiskers and eyebrows are short, brittle and tend to break very easily.

Colours and Patterns
All colours and patterns.

Eyes
All colours in keeping with coat colour.

Variation
Density and thickness of coat varies with age. Kittens often lose their waves and sometimes nearly all their coat around the time of teething so that it is never possible accurately to predict the type of adult coat other than in kittens who lack coat to the extent of appearing to be covered in suede. Such kittens are not suitable for the show bench although they make attractive pets. Coat subsequently varies in relation to hormone levels and nutrition.

Personality
Extrovert. A monkey in cat's clothing.

Voice
Variable. Sometimes quiet but at other times quite strident.

Kittens
Kittens open their eyes very early. Most kittens are born with definite wavy coats. The coat may virtually disappear at about five to six weeks of age, gradually regrowing as the kitten matures.

Show Status
First exhibited in England and granted recognition as a championship breed by the British GCCF in 1967. Granted recognition in the USA in 1972 except in CFA which included it in the same class as Cornish Rex until 1979. Shown in all countries of FIFe, USA, Canada and Japan.

Black smoke Devon Rex

Acknowledgements

My first thanks go to Pat Turner for her ineffable perception in judging my paintings, for allowing me to draw upon her vast knowledge, and contributing so much more than was ever originally envisaged; and Hilary Davies who read and imaginatively edited the manuscript. Equally I should like to thank Janet Smith for her tireless and enthusiastic assistance in the studio; Laura Smith who has been my photographic assistant whenever she could; John Barber for his constructive support and the painting of the Sphynx; and Christian Flood who so enthusiastically promoted my original ideas. I should also like to thank Liz Pitman who insisted on the best possible reproduction of the paintings, Adrian Morris who designed the book sensitively, and Michael Wright who kindly agreed to my using illustrations which first appeared in *The Book of the Cat* (Pan 1980) as breed introduction vignettes.

The following people helped with reference material in the form of cats or books, and I am very grateful to them: Pauline and Derrick Parsons for Snowshoes; Roslyn and Brian Copeland for Norwegian Forest Cats and Ragdolls; Miranda von Kirchberg for Russians; Angela Sayer Rixon for many cats, but especially Django and Oliver; Gunnar Ternsdedt for Norwegian Forest Cats; Barry Barber for Italian cat magazines; Marna Fogarty, Editor of the *Cat Fanciers' Association Yearbook*, for several *Yearbooks*; and Grace Pond for the National Cat Show; and all those who have so kindly allowed me to photograph their cats on show or at their homes.

Bibliography

Alderton, D., *The Cat*, Macdonald, London, 1983.

Angel, J., *Cats Kingdom*, Souvenir Press, London, 1985.

Ashford, A., and Pond, G., *Rex, Abyssinian and Turkish Cats*, Gifford, London, 1972.

Bloomfield, J., *Concise Dictionary of Cats*, Bison Books, London, 1977.

Bokonyi, S., *History of Domestic Animals in Central and Eastern Europe*, Akadémiai Kiadó, Budapest, 1974.

Boudreau, J. C., and Tsuchintani, C., *Sensory Neurophysiology*, Van Nostrand Reinhold, New York, 1973.

Brearley, J., *All About Himalayan Cats*, TFH, New Jersey, 1976.

Burton, J., and Allaby, M., *Nine Lives*, Ebury Press, London, 1985.

Clutton-Brock, J., *A Natural History of Domesticated Animals*, Cambridge University Press, Cambridge, 1981.

Clutton-Brock, J., *The British Museum Book of Cats*, British Museum, London, 1988.

Darwin, C., *Journal of Researches into the Natural History and Geology of the Countries Visited during the Voyage of HMS Beagle round the World*, Murray, London, 1860.

Darwin, C., *The Variation of Animals and Plants under Domestication*, Vol. 1, Murray, London, 1968.

Davis, S., *The Archaeology of Animals*, Batsford, London, 1987.

Dunnill, M., *The Siamese Owner's Encyclopaedia*, Pelham, London, 1974.

Ellenberger, Baum and Dittrich, *An Atlas of Animal Anatomy*, Dover, New York, 1949.

Epstein, H., *Domestic Animals of China*, Commonwealth Agricultural Bureau, London, 1969.

Eustace, M., *The World of Show Cats*, Pelham, London, 1970.

Fogarty, M. (ed.), *Cat Fancier's Association Yearbooks*, CFA, London, 1978, 1983, 1984, 1985, 1988–9.

Gambaryan, P. P., *How Mammals Run*, Wiley, New York, 1974.

Gilbert, S. G., *Pictorial Anatomy of the Cat*, University of Washington Press, Washington, 1968.

Hindley, J., *Siamese Cats Past and Present*, 1967.

Ing, C., and Pond, G., *Champion Cats*, Harrap, London, 1972.

Jennings, J., *Domestic and Fancy Cats*, Upcott Gill, 1985.

Kingdon, J., *East African Mammals*, Vol. IIIa, Academic Press, London, 1977.

Knystautas, A., *The Natural History of the USSR*, Century, London, 1987.

Lauder, P., *The Rex Cat*, David & Charles, Newton Abbot, 1974.

Leyhausen, P., *Cat Behaviour*, Garland, New York, 1979.

Maas, J-P., *Abessijen en Somalis*, Zuidgroep, Best, 1982.

Megaw, J., *Hunters, Gatherers and First Farmers Beyond Europe*, Leicester University Press, Leicester, 1975.

Meins, B., and Lloyd, W., *Show Your Cat*, TFH Publications, New Jersey, 1972.

Mery, F., *The Cat*, Hamlyn, London, 1967.

Mivart, St George, *The Cat*, Charles Scribner, New York, 1895.

Muybridge, E., *Animals in Motion*, Dover, New York, 1957.

Pintera, A., *Cats*, Hamlyn, London, 1988.

Pocock, R, et al, *The Burmese Cat*, Batsford, London, 1975.

Pond, G., *The Complete Cat Encyclopaedia*, Heinemann, London, 1972.

Pond, G., and Calder, M., *The Longhaired Cat*, Batsford, London, 1974.

Pugnetti, G., *The Macdonald Encyclopedia of Cats*, Macdonald, London, 1983.

Robinson, R., 'Cat', *Evolution of Domesticated Animals*, ed. I. L. Mason, Longman, London, 1984, 217–228.

Sacase, C., *The Cat*, Hamlyn, London, 1986.

Sayer, A., *Encyclopedia of the Cat*, Octopus, London, 1979.

Sayer, A., *The Complete Book of the Cat*, Hamlyn, London, 1988.

Simpson, F. (ed.), *The Book of the Cat*, Cassell, London, 1903.

Smith. V., *The Birman Cat*, privately published, 1980.

Sproule, A. and M., *Complete Cat Book*, Admiral, 1985.

Tabor, R., *The Wildlife of the Domestic Cat*, Arrow, London, 1983.

Taylor, D., *The Ultimate Cat Book*, Dorling Kindersley, London, 1989.

Tomkies, M., *Wildcat Haven*, Jonathan Cape, London, 1987.

Turner, P., 'The Breeds of Cats', *The Book of the Cat*, ed. M. Wright and S. Walters, Pan, London, 1979, 50–99.

Weir Harrison, *Our Cats*, 1889.

Wilson, M., *Encyclopaedia of American Cat Breeds*, TFH, New Jersey, 1978.

Wolfgang, H., *Ocelots and Margays*, TFH, New Jersey, 1964.

Wright, M., and Walters, S. (eds), *The Book of the Cat*, Pan, London, 1980.

Zeuner, *A History of Domesticated Animals*, Hutchinson, London, 1963.

Scientific Journals and Periodicals

Journal of Archaeological Science, 8, 1981.

Australian Journal of Zoology, 23, 1975.

Carnivore Genetics Newsletter, 1963–78.

Royal Zoological Society of London Proceedings, 1907, 1941, 1952.

Carnivore, 1, 1978.

Journal of Genetics, 1949, 1959.

Heredity, 1975.

Scientific American, 1977.

Mammalian Review, 1978.

Zoologicke Listy, 1976.

Cat Fancy Organizations

American Cat Association (ACA) 10065 Foothill Boulevard, Lakeview Terrace, California 91342, USA.
Offers a full pedigree registration service. Championship titles for pedigree breeds. Offers show classes for pet cats. Shows are organized in the USA style.

American Cat Fanciers Association (ACFA) PO Box 203 Point Lookout, Missouri 65726, USA.
As ACA

Canadian Cat Association (CCA) 14 Nelson Street West, Brampton, Ontario L6X 1BY, Canada.
As ACA

Cat Association of Britain (CA) Mill House, Letcombe Regis, OX12 9JD. Tel 02357 66543 and 0908 665373
Offers a full pedigree registration service, International and National Championship and Premiership titles for pedigree breeds; Laureate titles for non-pedigree cats; Medallist titles for provisionally accepted pedigree breeds and a cat welfare service (CARE). Has just become a member of FIFe at time of going to press. Shows are organized in the European style.

Cat Fanciers Association (CFA) 1309 Allaire Ave, Ocean, New Jersey, USA. Tel 201-531-2390.
As ACA

Cat Fanciers Federation (CFF) 1379 Tyler Park Drive, Louisville, Kentucky 40204, USA.
As ACA

Fédération Internationale Féline (FIFe) Boerhaavelaan 23.NL-5644 BB Eindhoven, the Netherlands. (Worldwide federation of member countries)
National clubs retain their independence but follow mutually agreed rules concerning the organization of national championship and international championship shows and the registration of cat pedigrees, and maintain lists of judges and cattery names recognized by all member countries. Shows are organized in the European style with national and international judges. A list of member clubs worldwide is available from the Secretariat.

Governing Council of the Cat Fancy (GCCF) 4–6 Penel Orlieu, Bridgwater, Somerset, TA6 3PG. Tel 0278 427575
Offers a registration service with full pedigrees supplied at extra cost. Offers national championships and premierships for pedigree breeds in Great Britain only. Maintains a list of British cattery names (called prefixes). Shows are organized in the pen judging style with the GCCF's own judges. Overseas judges are sometimes invited.

The International Cat Association (TICA) PO Box 2988, Harlingen, Texas 78551. Tel 512-428-8046.

United Cat Federation (UCF) 6621 Thornwood Street, San Diego, California 92111, USA.
As ACA

New Zealand Cat Fancies Inc. 20 Warren Kelly Street, Richmond, Nelson Tel 054 46721.
Contact Mrs Dee Shaw

Index